Mary Cadogan trained as a home economist at Croydon College after which she worked for a number of companies testing new products and developing recipes. She was assistant cookery editor on *Family Circle* for 2½ years. Her books include *Prepare to Cook, Salads, Casseroles, Good Home Baking, Romantic Italian Cookery* and *Salt Free Cookery* with Shirley Bond. She is married with two children.

Shirley Bond is a State Registered Dietitian, a member of the British Dietetic Association and a Fellow of the Institute of Home Economists. After working for several years as a dietitian in hospitals she worked as a nutrition lecturer in a college and then in the Department of Nutrition and Home Economics at the Flour Advisory Bureau, London. She now regularly writes on food, nutrition and diets for magazines, newspapers and food manufacturers. Her books include *Eat and Be Fit* and *Salt Free Cookery* with Mary Cadogan. She is married with two children.

✸ POSITIVE HEALTH GUIDE

THE OAT COOKBOOK

Mary Cadogan
and
Shirley Bond

O P T I M A

© Mary Cadogan and Shirley Bond 1987

First published in 1987 by
Macdonald Optima, a division of
Macdonald & Co. (Publishers) Ltd

Conceived and edited by Martin Dunitz Ltd
154 Camden High Street
London NW1 0NE

British Library Cataloguing in Publication Data

Cadogan, Mary
    The oat cookbook.
    1. Cookery (Oats)
    I. Title   II. Bond, Shirley
    641.6'313   TX809.02

    ISBN 0-356-15238-3

Macdonald & Co. (Publishers) Ltd
3rd floor
Greater London House
Hampstead Road
London NW1 7QX

Phototypeset by BookEns, Saffron Walden, Essex
Printed in Singapore by Toppan Printing Company (S) Pte Ltd

CONTENTS

INTRODUCTION

We eat because we get hungry, because we like food and we need it to keep fit. But that's not all there is to it. In recent years people have started to become aware that food plays a vital part in health. There can be few now who have not wondered whether their choice of food, in both quantity and quality, couldn't perhaps be more suitable for their needs, and make them fitter now and in the years to come. Unfortunately it can be difficult to know which foods to eat and which to avoid.

Most foods will satisfy hunger pangs and we all have our special likes and dislikes. Our choice may depend on what our parents brought us up to eat, our culture and its food customs, what food is available at the time we are hungry, and what food we can afford to buy and have the facilities to cook. But the prime consideration when choosing between one food and another should be nutritional value.

Analysing food values each mealtime is impracticable because it is difficult and time-consuming, but to have an idea of which foods are nutritious, which to avoid, the good and the not-so-good cooking methods, and which combinations of foods provide extra food value is of immense value in following a healthy eating pattern. Many people who have changed their choice of food, even by just a little, have felt so much fitter that they are not in the least tempted to return to some of the foods they used to eat in large quantities. Drastic overnight changes are not necessary, neither is eating foods you don't like just because they contain a particular vitamin. The key is to enjoy food in as wide a variety as possible but consider carefully what you are eating and choose for health as well as taste.

Healthy eating guidelines
In 1983 and 1984 two important documents were published – one by the Committee on Medical Aspects of Food Policy (COMA) and one by the National Advisory Committee on Nutrition Education (NACNE). The recommendations of both bodies were very similar; that we should follow these guidelines:

- Increase our intake of starchy carbohydrate.
- Increase our intake of dietary fibre.
- Increase our intake of fruit and vegetables.
- Reduce our average intake of sugar.
- Reduce our average intake of total fat, cutting right down on saturated fats (which are most animal fats) and substituting polyunsaturated fats.
- Reduce our average intake of salt.

- Reduce our average intake of alcohol, that is, drink only in moderation.
- Alter our intake of protein so that we get more from cereal and plant sources and less from animal sources.

With these reliable guidelines it is now possible to look at different foods and consider the part they play in the nation's diet, in individual diets and in therapeutic diets. We can judge how the food measures up to the recommendations in these reports. In this book you will see the part that oats have played in the nation's diet over the centuries and how they fit so well into the recommendations for healthy eating today. There are also 150 recipes to show how you can use oats in everyday cooking with delicious results.

History and cultivation

Oats were one of the earliest cereals cultivated by man. They were known in ancient China as long ago as 7000 BC while the Greeks are the first people known to have made a recognizable porridge from oats. It was the Romans who not only introduced oats to other countries in Europe, but also gave them and other cultivated grasses the name cereals, after Ceres, the Roman goddess of agriculture.

Wheat and barley were the first cereals to be cultivated. The seed was kept from one year to be sown the following year but because there was no way of thoroughly cleaning and selecting the seed, each crop contained a proportion of weeds. As the cultivation of cereals spread to the damper climate of north-west Europe, two of the 'weeds' started to grow more successfully than the wheat and barley. In the cool, moist conditions, oats and rye thrived and became cereal crops in their own right. Rye was cultivated more widely in the Scandinavian countries, where it is still popular today, and the common oat (*Avena sativa*) derived from the western Asian wild grass (*Avena fatua*), took its place beside wheat and barley as the main cereal crops in Britain.

Early varieties of oats grew best in a cool climate with early summer rain that allowed the kernel to develop gradually. In the UK, Scotland, the north of England and Northern Ireland had the most suitable climate for growing oats and by the sixth century oats were established in Scotland alongside barley as a popular cereal crop. The Romans called the cereal they had introduced, food for the savages of Northern Europe. The fact that oat grains have been found in archaeological remains all over England, and that there are many Celtic, old Nordic and old Germanic names for oats shows how well their 'product' took off.

The easy preparation of oats also encouraged their early use. In

1327 the French chronicler Froissart noted that, on their journeys into England, Scottish soldiers never bothered with pots and pans, but seemed content to ride with a bag of oatmeal and a flat stone strapped between the saddle and the saddle cloth. When they got tired of a diet of stolen cattle they mixed up a paste of oatmeal and water and made little cakes, cooked on the stone among the camp-fire embers.

Oats – in and out of favour

For centuries nutritious, cheap oats were the staple food for those living in the poorest conditions in Europe. Then around 1770, through the introduction of the potato, oats were usurped and instead used more and more as food for horses and cattle. In Scotland they remained popular. In Johnson's *Dictionary of the English Language* published in 1755 appeared the now famous definition of oats: 'A grain which in England is generally given to horses, but in Scotland supports the people.' The reason for this was probably that grass was rich and plentiful in Scotland and domestic animals did not need their feeding supplemented as much.

By the end of the sixteenth century oats were quoted as a crop in the feudal equivalent of the Corn Exchange and, by the beginning of the nineteenth century, similar acreages of wheat, barley and oats were grown in Britain. Wheat became the favoured cereal for bread-making because of its high gluten content, which is necessary to give a loaf a good shape, structure and texture and barley crops were used predominantly for malting and brewing. Oats could take the place of wheat and barley if they were not available, but the final baked and brewed oat products were inferior and not generally acceptable.

In the eighteenth and nineteenth centuries the traditional strains of Scottish oats were crossed with imported oats from the Continent and gradually since then high-yielding strains of oats for growth in particular areas and varying climatic conditions have been developed, including a variety of red oat (*Avena byzantina*) which is adapted to hot climates and is grown in America and Mediterranean countries. Even so, during the twentieth century the amount grown began to decline. This was perhaps partly because less oats were needed to feed horses as horses were gradually replaced by tractors and motor cars, and partly because the increasingly affluent turned from eating cereals towards more meat and dairy foods.

With the increased interest in health and preventive medicine, oats are now back in favour. They satisfy the criteria for good eating as well as being a useful ingredient in many delicious recipes. Our ancestors knew by instinct that eating oats would help to keep them healthy. Modern medical research has proved them right.

From field to miller

Today's many varieties of oats have evolved through the centuries from wild grass. Best quality oats are grown on light, fertile soil and will grow in most regions with a temperate climate and a rainfall of over 60 cm (24 in) a year. The main oat-producing areas are the USA, Canada, USSR, West Germany, France, Australia and Scandinavia; England and Scotland are secondary producers.

The oat grain is grown and ripened in the fields and goes straight from the field to the oat miller. You can recognize a field of oats by the way the grains appear in clusters called panicles on graceful nodding stems. An oat plant grows to around 90 cm (3 ft) high and each stem carries about twenty to twenty-five oat grains. Each panicle carries two or three grains and each grain is covered by its husk that protects it all the way to the mill.

To the farmer these grains can be the seed for the following year's crop. To the oat miller the grains, subjected to his milling techniques, are the raw material for a great variety of oat cereal products.

Cleaning and sorting   When the oats arrive at the mill from a farm they contain impurities such as soil, seeds, sticks, stones, straw and pieces of metal. Different machines remove these impurities by passing the oats over magnets, by sieving and by aspiration (blowing away). Other mechanical machines, such as high-capacity cylinders and indented discs, sort out the oats by picking up and removing the small grains or seeds and leaving behind the larger oats to be milled.

The oat plant, or panicle

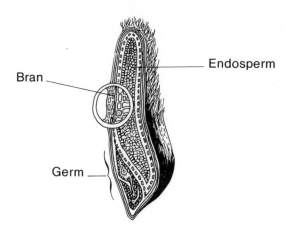

The oat grain

Stabilization Oats contain various enzymes, one of which is lipase. If this is not neutralized during milling, a large amount of undesirable free fatty acids may be present in the packaged oatmeal. These break down the fat in the oatflakes and can produce a bitter, rancid taste. So the enzyme has to be destroyed by a stabilizing process. This involves both steaming and drying.

Steaming Stabilization by steaming involves quickly raising the temperature of the oats to 96°C to 100°C (205°F to 212°F) by injecting steam at atmospheric pressure. The oat grains are held at that temperature for two to three minutes. Almost all the lipase is in the pericarp, the outer layer of the kernel, so this external treatment doesn't affect the inside of the grain or its nutritional value. In fact, this treatment, besides inactivating the lipase, has an enhancing effect on the flavour of the oats. This is one of the most vital parts of the milling process and millers have to take great care to avoid excessive steaming. Too much can result in the fat oxidizing, which can cause rancidity.

Drying or kilning The natural moisture content of oats after cleaning is around 12 to 16 per cent. To make milling easier, the grain must be dried to about 6 per cent moisture content.
You can still see traditional methods of kilning (drying) in crofts in remote areas of Scotland. In fact in Scotland, until around 1850, farmers supervised their own kilning. Most were very knowledgeable but the miller could get better quality results with greater efficiency. Today there are so many different varieties of oats, all of differing qualities and requiring different milling techniques, and the quantities involved are so large, that modern

milling is virtually essential, although some say that oats prepared in the old-fashioned way had the best flavour of all.

Modern kilning is a continuous drying process where hot air is drawn through the oats as they pass slowly down a column. If the oats are to be stored, they need a moisture content of 12 per cent. If the final milling is to take place immediately, the oats need to be given a final drying at a temperature of 80°C (175°F) to make the hull of each grain brittle and easier to remove. The oats are also given a final 'roasting' at 150°C (300°F) to bring the moisture content down to the required 6 per cent and enhance the nutty flavour.

Correct kilning is vital – overdrying will produce an undesirable flavour, while underdrying will prevent any flavour at all coming through. After this initial preparation, the whole oat grain is ready to be milled into its component parts and treated in a variety of ways before being packaged for the consumer.

Hulling or shelling   Each grain is partially enclosed in two thin papery husks or chaff called the **hull**. This outer skin is tough and fibrous and mostly consists of crude fibre. It must be removed before further processing can continue. To do this the oat is thrown at very high speed against a stationary rubber surface to spring the kernel or groat from the shell, before the whole lot passes over an aspirator which blows away the lighter-density oat husk. Any unshelled oats that get through are returned to the shelling process.

At this stage the oats are called **groats** and they pass on through the mill for further processing. Beneath the hull are the layers of **bran** – two thin layers which are rich in soluble dietary fibre. These may be removed to form the product **oat bran** or they may be removed along with the germ to form the product **oat bran and oat germ** or may be left on the groat to pass through the mill.

Polishing   The groats have fine hairs covered in little particles of oat dust, which is loosened by brushing or scouring and removed by sieving or aspiration.

Cutting   The brushed groats are cut on rotary granulators into three pieces. Aspiration again removes any remaining oat husk and any flour from this cutting process is removed and used for animal food products. These cut groats are called **pinhead oatmeal**. From this cleaned, milled, pinhead oatmeal you get several varieties of oatmeal products, such as **medium oatmeal, fine oatmeal** and **oatflour**.

Steaming and flaking   If the groats are flaked, cooked, rolled and dried they form large flakes and are sold as **jumbo oats**. Pinhead oatmeal may be softened by steam then flattened on flaking rollers. The steaming partially cooks the oats and this, together with the finer rolling, means the resulting **rolled oats, oat flakes** or **flaked oats** cook more quickly and are easier to digest than the pinhead oatmeal.

At all stages, extremely careful checks are made to make sure no strange seeds, lead shot, minute stones or other particles pass into the final product. Each miller manufactures his products in a slightly different way but whichever order the processing follows, nothing is detracted from the nutritional value of the oats. It is this minimal processing that makes oats such a nutritious and adaptable commodity.

Oat products

Through all the stages of the milling process, oat products are obtained. They can be sold as they are, for instance as a packet of jumbo oats, or they can be combined in numerous ways to make many different products, such as muesli. By reading the packet, you can check the contents so that you buy the oats in the correct form for your needs.

- **Hull or husk** is not suitable for human consumption so is ground down and used for cattle food.

- **Groats** often used to be pounded down to make a **very** coarse oatmeal but it had a rough texture and was quite indigestible. It is possible to buy groats in specialist shops, sometimes mixed with brown rice and seeds, but they require a lot of soaking and cooking before they are palatable and easy to digest.

- **Oat bran** is occasionally sold as a separate product. It can be used on its own to make a hot cereal dish like porridge or mixed in with other oat products such as rolled oats to enhance their fibre value. In some recipes it may be mixed with cereals such as wheat flour and used in baking.

- **Oat bran and oat germ** are usually sold together as an oat product unless the whole groat is milled without having any part removed. If the whole groat is milled, the bran is interspersed throughout the resulting oatmeal products.

- **Pinhead oatmeal** is coarse in texture but can be made into delicious, traditional Scottish porridge which is more granular than the porridge most people are accustomed to. Those who find it too coarse may prefer pre-cooked, pinhead oatmeal, available in various forms of oatflakes. Pinhead oatmeal can be ideal for adding texture as well as nutritional value to soups, stews and toppings for pies and puddings.

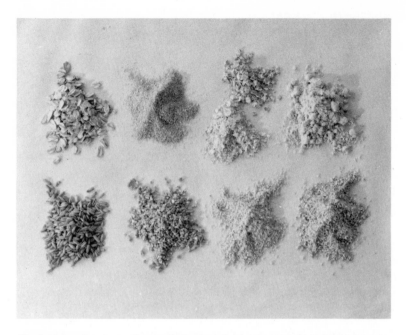

Varieties of oat products: *left to right, top row* jumbo oats, oatbran and oatgerm, rolled and thin rolled oats, oat flour; *bottom row* groats, pinhead oatmeal, fine oatmeal, medium oatmeal.

- **Jumbo oats** are the largest variety of flaked oatmeal and ideal for making a good thick porridge. They have quite a nutty flavour and are ideal for biscuit making.

- **Rolled oats** (porridge oats) are sometimes called oatflakes, Superfast oats or quick and easy oats. They cook more quickly than Jumbo oats as they are partially cooked during the milling process. They are still fairly coarse compared to oatflour and are ideal for porridge, muesli, parkin and flapjack biscuits.

- **Medium oatmeal** has a pleasant slightly rough texture, ideal for porridge, oatcakes and parkin. It is the best variety for coating fish and meat before frying and is good in stuffings and crumble toppings.

- **Fine oatmeal** makes a lovely smooth milk pudding. This is the type to use as a thickening agent for soups, sauces and gravy.

- **Oat flour** is a very fine, smooth-textured flour. It is ideal baby food and is also good as a thickening agent. Mixed with wheat-flour it is delicious in biscuits, bread, cakes, scones and pastry.

Why eat oats?

Oats and carbohydrate

There are many ways in which you can use oats to meet the recommendations for healthy eating. In particular, they are an excellent source of starchy carbohydrate and soluble dietary fibre. The COMA report says, 'It would be advantageous to increase the intake of fibre-rich carbohydrates (bread, cereals, fruit and vegetables) providing this can be achieved without increasing total intake of common salt or simple sugars.'

Carbohydrate at present provides about 42 per cent of the calories in the average British diet and comes in the form of sugar and starch. All carbohydrates in excess can cause overweight. The particular drawback of sugar is that it provides calories (energy) but no other nutrients. It causes tooth decay and it is very easy to eat too much because sugar has no bulk.

There are two kinds of starch, refined and unrefined. Refined starchy foods include white bread and flour and white rice. These foods lack the fibre and some of the nutrients of unrefined cereals. Unrefined cereals, which we should be eating more of, include wholemeal cereals, oat products, pulses and seeds. Their special advantage is that they have not lost any nutrients to refining, and their natural fibre gives them filling but non-fattening bulk.

Since the end of the Second World War the population has generally become more affluent and therefore people have tended to buy more meat, sweets, convenience foods and dairy products. The amount of cereal foods, such as oats, in the diet has declined and obesity has become a problem for many. As the fashion for slimming grew, slimmers omitted the starchy foods from their diet, believing them to be the villains. We now realize that unrefined carbohydrates are desirable for health. Besides energy they give us protein, dietary fibre, minerals and vitamins. As we reduce our intake of foods containing fat and sugar, we should make up the energy shortfall by eating more unrefined starch.

We would be well advised to plan our meals as they do in countries such as Japan and China. They think of the cereal content as the base for a meal, then add fresh fruit and/or vegetables and, last, smaller amounts of meat, more as a garnish and for added flavour than anything else. Wholemeal flour and pasta, oatmeal in all its forms, jacket potatoes and brown rice can all form a good starchy-carbohydrate, high-dietary-fibre base on which to build a meal or a recipe. Carbohydrate should provide at least 55 per cent of our daily calorie requirement.

As the guidelines point out, the extra starch carbohydrate must not be accompanied by an increase in sugar or salt. The recipes in this book have been written with this in mind and salt and sugar are kept to a minimum.

Oats and dietary fibre

The COMA report also suggests the total amount of dietary fibre in the diet should be increased by using more unrefined cereals (wholewheat products, oatmeal products and brown rice), using pulses instead of and as well as meat, and more fruit and vegetables.

Dietary fibre has no nutritional value but it is a vitally important part of our diet. It used to be called roughage and its part in the diet was greatly underestimated. In fact everything seems to have been done to avoid eating it. White bread was more popular than brown so the wheat bran and germ were removed from flour during milling. Oatmeal lost favour and was given more to horses than humans. Fruit and vegetables were usually peeled, cored and cooked to make them softer. More and more plant foods were processed so that the fibre, which is mostly found in the outer skin and cell walls, was removed.

Then scientists, looking at the relationship between diseases and diet in many countries, began to realize that in countries where people ate a high-fibre diet, the incidence of constipation and cancer of the colon was much less. They began to see that for better health the average British diet should contain more total dietary fibre. Besides the complaints already mentioned, fibre may play a part in preventing diverticular disease, late-onset diabetes, obesity, haemorrhoids, varicose veins and appendicitis. Even high blood cholesterol levels, leading to coronary heart disease, can sometimes be lowered by eating more fibre.

Fibre is formed from a mixture of substances; cellulose and hemi-cellulose which are polysaccharides, lignin which is the woody part of plants, and gum and pectin which are in the soft tissues of fruits and vegetables. Cereal fibre in particular should be increased because it is more effective than fruit and vegetable fibre.

Further research has shown that there are two main types of dietary fibre and both are necessary in the diet.

Water-insoluble fibre, such as cellulose found in the plant cell walls of foods, cannot be digested by the body. (Bran is water-insoluble fibre.) It absorbs water and adds bulk to the body's waste material. This bulk is very important. It stimulates the muscular contractions which move food steadily along the intestine so that all its nutritive value is derived and the waste is easily evacuated.

Without this fibre the faeces do not absorb water. They are hard and tend to remain in the large intestine for longer than they should. This causes irritations such as diverticulitis, constipation, haemorrhoids and appendicitis.

It is best to take insoluble fibre into the body in the form it naturally occurs in food, such as in wholemeal bread and cereals, kidney beans and pulses and nuts. It is not wise to eat more refined food and then sprinkle bran on to everything as this can sometimes be excessive and cause abdominal discomfort.

Soluble fibre is partially broken down during digestion and plays a valuable part in some of the body's metabolic processes. Oats are particularly rich in soluble fibre. The part of the oat that has the highest concentration of soluble fibre is the bran, but tests have shown that any oat product eaten in sufficient quantity will be beneficial. The soluble fibre in oats has been shown to reduce the blood cholesterol level. This can be useful for those suffering from hypercholesterolaemia – too high blood cholesterol (see page 23) – although not all patients respond to changes in diet.

It also affects the blood sugar level, an important factor in controlling diabetes (see page 22).

There are two other benefits from a high-fibre diet. Fibrous foods are filling so you eat less of them, especially helpful for slimmers as they make them feel full, and they require extra chewing which helps to improve dental health.

The body needs both soluble and insoluble fibre. Oats are one of the richest and most easily available sources of soluble fibre so including them in the diet on a regular basis is very beneficial to health.

Oats for protein

The report states that it would do no harm for most people to eat a little less protein. It is recommended that a larger percentage of our protein should come from cereals, pulses and nuts rather than animal sources.

This recommendation does not just consider the amount of protein in the diet, but the foods from which it comes. Many animal protein sources are high in total fat, especially saturated fat. By eating more cereal and vegetable protein instead, you reduce your intake of fat and increase your intake of starchy carbohydrate and dietary fibre.

Protein is essential for the healthy growth of all body tissues. It is especially important for babies and growing children, during pregnancy, after operations and any time that new tissue is being formed. It is also needed by everyone, everyday, to replace worn-out tissues and to make blood cells, hormones and enzymes in the body.

Proteins are made up of units called amino acids. There are many different amino acids but only ten are essential for children and eight are essential for adults. The quality of any protein depends on its amino acid content. Animal proteins such as meat, fish, eggs and milk products contain the essential amino acids in the right proportions. They are said to be of high biological value. Cereal and vegetable proteins are usually deficient in one or two essential amino acids, therefore they are of lower biological value.

To overcome these deficiencies you need to combine a vegetable protein with an animal protein, or combine two vegetable

Amino acid content of some foods (mg/g protein)

Essential amino acids	Requirement	Oat-flakes	Wheat-meal	Rice	Maize	Leguminous plants	Milk powder	Beef
isoleucine	40	41	40	51	27	43	52	53
leucine	70	78	77	94	94	68	97	82
lysine	55	40	23	37	20	75	71	87
methionine and cystine	35	47	44	55	29	35	35	38
phenylalanine and tyrosine	60	89	79	109	65	73	96	75
threonine	40	36	29	48	26	41	41	43
tryptophan	10	14	12	12	7	9	14	12
valine	50	55	45	78	33	47	63	55

The requirement figure refers to the amount required by young children and will therefore be sufficient for older children and adults.
(Figures taken from the recommendations of WHO/FAO.)

proteins. These protein 'mixes' are usually of far better total nutritional value than a single plant protein source. For example, as you can see in the chart above, oatflakes do not supply quite enough of the amino acid lysine. Lysine in this case is what is called a limiting amino acid. But milk is high in lysine so by making, for instance, milky porridge, you have an ideal protein dish.

Through the ages, oats have provided a very large percentage of the diet's protein requirement. They are rich in protein – 13 per cent. But whereas the nation's diet once relied on cereals as a base, during the last two centuries proteins of animal origin have become more popular. With the swing back to cereals, oats will again play an important part in providing the essential amino acids in the diet.

Oats and fat
The COMA report recommends that: 'there should be a reduction in the average total fat content of the diet to the level at which it provides at the most 34 per cent of total calorie intake and preferably less to 30 per cent of total calorie/joule intake. The reduction should come from saturated fats; the polyunsaturated fats should not be reduced, indeed some are essential in the diet.'

It is easy to assume from their floury appearance that cereals, including oats, do not contain any fat. In fact oats contain 8.7 per cent fat, made up of the three main types, saturated, monounsaturated and polyunsaturated.

To cut down on saturated fats you should avoid frying, spread fats thinly on bread, use skimmed or semi-skimmed milk, and avoid fat in meat and in processed foods, both savoury and sweet. Polyunsaturated fatty acids, on the other hand, may be eaten in moderation. They are beneficial, especially the two essential fatty acids, linoleic and linolenic. Oats contain a very small amount of saturated fat but provide good quantities of the essential fatty acids.

When using oats in recipes requiring fat, remember to use other polyunsaturated fats, such as margarines high in polyunsaturates, and oils such as soya and sunflower, rather than animal fats such as lard, butter and ordinary margarines. Olive oil, which is mono-unsaturated, is also suitable. Avoid palm and coconut oil, however, as these are the two vegetable oils that are high in saturated fats.

Oats and sugar

The COMA panel recommends that the intake of simple sugars sucrose, glucose and fructose should not be increased further.

There are several reasons for this recommendation. A large percentage of the population is overweight (see page 21) and this is partly because of the large quantity of sweet foods we eat. Foods containing sugar are often those that also contribute saturated fatty acids to the diet (see above) in the form of cakes, biscuits and puddings. Sweet foods can lead to dental decay too, particularly damaging to the young. Sugar is most harmful taken between meals, when it gets the chance to linger on the teeth.

Oats, however, are free of sugars and none is added during milling. If you want sweetness in an oats dish, such as muesli, dried or fresh fruit will add minerals, vitamins and dietary fibre as well as sweetness. Everyone should aim to reduce sugar intake until it supplies only around 10 per cent of total calorie (energy) intake.

Oats and salt

The COMA report recommends that: 'the dietary intake of common salt should not be increased further and that consideration should be given to ways and means of decreasing it.'

Common salt is sodium chloride and the sodium part of the compound has been linked to the possible cause of high blood pressure and heart disease. It is estimated that in the UK each person takes approximately 7–10 g salt each day. Much of this is added during cooking or at the table, and a further large proportion is added by manufacturers to food. Only a small amount occurs naturally in foods.

We need only around 3 g of salt a day. In some people, eating too much salt leads to high blood pressure which can, in turn, lead to heart attacks and strokes. There is no way of telling for certain which people are likely to be most affected, but those with a history of high blood pressure in the family are certainly thought to be at risk. While further research is taking place it is recommended that everyone should take less salt to be on the safe side.

The nutritive value of oatmeal

	Nutrients in 100 g raw oatmeal
Kilocalories	401
K joules	1698
Protein	12.4 g
Fat	8.7 g
Carbohydrate	72.8 g
Calcium	55 mg
Phosphorus	380 mg
Potassium	370 mg
Sodium	33 mg
Iron	4.1 mg
Thiamine	0.50 mg
Riboflavine	0.10 mg
Nicotinic acid	1.0 mg
Copper	0.23 mg
Zinc	(3.0) mg
Magnesium	110 mg
Vitamin B_6	0.12 mg
Vitamin B_{12}	0 mg
Folic acid	60 μg
Pantothenic acid	0.1 mg
Biotin	20 μg
Soluble dietary fibre	3.7 g
Insoluble dietary fibre	2.9 g
Total dietary fibre	6.6 g

Oats have naturally a very small amount of sodium – 33 mg per 100 g (9 mg per ounce) – so they add only a very small amount of sodium to any recipe. However, you should take care not to add salt to oat recipes and to use herbs, spices, dried fruit and fresh fruit for flavourings instead. These help bring out the real flavour of the oats, too.

Traditionally porridge is made with salt, not sugar – indeed many Scots consider salt is the only permissible addition. If you like salt on porridge, try adding a small pinch and stirring it in before considering adding more. You may find that you don't need more – and be able gradually to cut down from there.

Oats for vitamins and minerals
Oats are a valuable source of many vitamins, especially those in the B-complex. As the whole grain is used in the manufacture of oatmeal, there is no loss of vitamins and minerals.

Vitamin B_1 (thiamin) is partly destroyed when heated, such as in the baking of bread. During the milling of oatflakes there is no loss of vitamin B_1. This vitamin aids in the conversion of carbohydrate into energy in the muscles.

Vitamin B$_2$ (riboflavin) is heat resistant but susceptible to light. There is minimal loss when oats are used in a recipe. It is essential for normal health and growth and in the digestion of nutrients.

Vitamin B$_3$ (nicotinic acid) is essential in the diet. It can be made in the body from the amino acid tryptophan. As oats are rich in tryptophan they are an especially good source of this vitamin. It is necessary for healthy nerves, skin and digestive system.

Vitamin B$_6$ (pyrodoxine) is found in the outer layers of grains. It helps the body to assimilate protein and keeps the muscles, nerves and skin healthy.

Vitamin E occurs in small quantities in a wide variety of foods. It seems essential for a variety of functions in the body but its precise function is not known. Its natural presence in oats certainly serves a very useful purpose in preventing the oxidation of the poly-unsaturated fatty acids.

Minerals Calcium, iron and phosphorus are provided in good quantity by oats. These are not destroyed during milling and are very beneficial to people of all ages, especially the very young child and the old person. Compared to other cereals, oats are rich sources of zinc and manganese too.

It has been said that eating high quantities of oats can hinder the absorption of calcium because of the phytic acid they contain. However recent research has shown that an enzyme in the intestine effectively deals with the phytic acid so that it is not a problem.

Slimming and special diets

The COMA report states that: 'Obesity should be avoided both in adults and in children by a combination of appropriate food intake and regular exercise. Those who are overweight are advised to adjust food intake in relation to physical activity until their weight is within the acceptable range as defined in a report of the Royal College of Physicians.'

There has been a progressive increase in the average weight-for-height of adults in Britain over the last forty years and it is said that 40 per cent of middle-aged men and women are overweight. This is attributed to a decline in physical activity and a diet rich in fat and sugar with not enough dietary fibre.

Would-be slimmers often think that if they totally exclude certain foods from their diet they will lose weight. The first foods to go are often cereals, bread and potatoes as they still have a fattening image. Yet these should be among the last foods to go because their nutritional contribution is very high. Dietitians and doctors generally agree that the best way to slim and keep healthy at the same time, which is of course vitally important, is to cut right down on the fat and sugar intake, raise the dietary fibre intake, count calories and do more exercise.

The general healthy-eating guidelines given in this book are ideal for slimmers as well as those of correct weight, but if you are slimming you should eat portion sizes to fit with your calorie allowance. Oats fit easily into a slimming diet and the recipes in this book are all calorie counted. For instance, raw oatmeal is not high in calories: 100 g/4 oz provide 401 kilocalories, 1698 K joules, and 25 g/1 oz 114 kilocalories, 478 K joules.

Porridge made the traditional way with water, using 12.5 g/½ oz oatmeal, provides 57 kilocalories, 238 K joules. One portion of porridge made with 12.5 g/½ oz oatmeal and 150 ml/¼ pint milk provides 147 kilocalories, 614 K joules. If you like milk with porridge but are counting the calories, use skimmed milk, which cuts the total kilocalories in the porridge to 66 per serving, or 275 K joules.

Half a small carton of low-fat natural yoghurt tastes good with porridge and provides a total of 95 kilocalories, 410 K joules. Don't add sugar or honey – try a little bit of fresh fruit instead. Similar reductions can be made if an oat-based muesli is preferred.

Any slimmer can enjoy a nourishing breakfast of porridge or muesli and can cook freely with oats. The dietary fibre in oats is especially useful for slimmers. It satisfies hunger and keeps the digestive system healthy. Just take care, if you are slimming, over the foods you choose to cook or eat with the oats.

Oats and diabetes

Diabetes is caused by an excess of sugar in the bloodstream. Normally the body can control its own balance between the sugar eaten and the sugar made in the body. When it can't, the usual treatment is by special diet, sometimes by medication, and if the control is entirely lost, by regular insulin injections.

Diabetes is much less common among populations eating a high-fibre diet than in Western countries such as Britain which generally have a low-fibre intake. A diet high in soluble fibre can help in weight control too (see above). Many diabetics who are not on insulin have a weight problem, so eating plenty of soluble fibre, reducing fat and sugar and increasing exercise, can help them to control their problems – both weight and diabetic – without insulin.

The soluble fibre also smooths out the blood sugar by slowing down its absorption. This has a very beneficial effect on the health of insulin-dependent diabetics too, who in some cases have lowered their blood sugar levels and reduced their insulin requirements. It is very important, however, that people with diabetes should not alter their insulin or diet themselves but should consult their doctor and dietitian who will make the necessary adjustments.

Oats and cholesterol

The COMA panel stated, 'there are no specific recommendations about the dietary intake of cholesterol.'

They felt that if the intake of saturated fat was reduced, then the intake of cholesterol would be likely to fall too.

Eighty per cent of the cholesterol in the body is made by the body itself and this you can do nothing about. Cholesterol's main function is to produce bile in the liver. If the level of cholesterol in the blood falls too low then the body will produce more to keep up the production of bile.

Twenty per cent of the cholesterol is taken in as food and if you eat too much, the blood cholesterol level can become too high. It is found in varying amounts in animal foods, especially egg yolks, offal and animal products such as butter, lard and suet. There is almost no cholesterol in cereals, vegetables or fruit.

Too much cholesterol can lead to hardening and blocking of the arteries and to coronary attacks and heart disease. So to reduce the likelihood of heart disease especially if you have a family history of heart trouble, it may be helpful to regulate your blood cholesterol level, primarily by cutting down on saturated fats. It also helps to have a diet high in soluble fibre because oats and other foods rich in water-soluble fibre have been shown to lower the cholesterol levels in the blood. It seems that the soluble fibre increases the loss of bile acids in the faeces. As the bile acids are formed from cholesterol, the cholesterol is diverted towards making more bile acids rather than staying in circulation and causing trouble by blocking arteries.

The combined effects of loss of cholesterol in the faeces and less cholesterol being made by the body, lower the blood cholesterol. Oat products and pulses are especially effective because they are the richest sources of soluble fibre. Eating them regularly keeps blood cholesterol under control and can even lower it by as much as 30 per cent.

Oats and coeliac disease

Anyone suffering from coeliac disease is unable to tolerate gluten, a substance that is high, for example, in wheat. This means avoiding many cereal-based products unless they are made from special gluten-free flour.

Oats contain minute amounts of gluten compared to wheat and many coeliac patients are able to tolerate oats in their diet. However, there are many who cannot, and those suffering from coeliac disease or an intolerance to gluten should not use oats until their doctor or dietitian has specifically tested them for any adverse reaction and advised them accordingly.

Oats and allergies

If you are allergic to one or more of the many pesticides, additives, preservatives, colourings or flavourings used in the processing and manufacturing of many foods, you may wonder what treatment oatmeal has in its passage from the field to the supermarket shelf.

The news is good. Pesticides used on fields of oats are unable to get through to the groat, the part of the oat that is milled and eaten, because even the valuable bran layers on the outside of the groat are protected by the layer of inedible husk which is discarded.

No additives, no salt or sugar or any other preservatives, are added to oatmeal. The only additions made to oats are to one or two brands of 'instant' hot oat cereal which have extra iron and vitamins added. Details of these are usually on the side of the packet. The consumer can decide whether to use the oats for a savoury or sweet recipe, and what flavourings to add.

The versatility of oats in cooking, along with the fact that they are unrefined, nutritious, and cheap to buy, are what make them an ideal staple in today's diet.

THE RECIPES

Oats are often considered to be good for making porridge, but little else. If this is your view, then think again. Oats in their many forms, from fine oatmeal to jumbo oats, can add their nutty texture and homely flavour to countless dishes. They are cheap, easy to use, quick to cook and readily available.

- Use them as you would breadcrumbs to coat, bind, sprinkle and bulk.
- Toast them for using in salads and with vegetables.
- Their naturally sweet taste is excellent for cakes, puddings and biscuits.
- Rolled oats are useful for last-minute thickening of soups, sauces and gravy. Simply sprinkle a handful into the liquid and simmer for five minutes.

Use oats freely as they are good for you, providing much fibre as well as protein, vitamins and minerals. We hope you will enjoy trying the recipes in this book, which are devised to give you good food that will keep you in good health.

Buying and storing oats
It is advisable to buy oats in the most suitable form for the cooking you intend to do (see page 13), but you can make your own oatmeal, as fine as you wish, by putting rolled oats in a food processor or blender for a minute or two.

At one time people were wary of buying oats in large quantities because they could go rancid before being used up. Rancidity was caused by the enzyme, lipase, which breaks down the fat in the oats and produces a bitter taste. Now the steaming process to which the oats are subjected during milling destroys this enzyme, and modern millers make sure this stabilization process is accurate. So you can store oats for many months without deterioration in quality, although once a packet is opened it is best to use them within a few months. You will find a 'best before' date on each packet, but they will almost certainly be quite safe to eat after that day.

As with other cereal products, oats are liable to attack by weevils, mice or insects. They should be stored in dry, cool conditions with adequate ventilation. Once a packet is opened, transfer the oats to a screw-top jar and label it according to type. When the jar is nearly empty, remove the old oatmeal and clean the jar before filling with new oatmeal and replacing the older oatmeal on top.

Cleaning the porridge pan
People often hesitate to make porridge on account of the sticky pans. In fact, washing up your porridge pan is not a problem. Soak it for thirty minutes in cold water after use. Cleaning will then be easy as oats are non-greasy.

Measurements
Ingredients are given in both metric and imperial measures. Use either set of quantities, but not a mixture of both in any one recipe.

All spoon measurements are level unless otherwise stated. Standard measuring spoons are useful for complete accuracy:

> 1 tsp (teaspoon) = 5 ml
> 1 tbsp (tablespoon) = 15 ml

Eggs are size 3 unless otherwise stated.

Fibre   To our knowledge, this is the first oat cookery book to include the correct figures for both soluble and insoluble fibre in the dietary analyses for each recipe. To achieve the total fibre figure you have simply to add the two separate fibre figures together.

Cooking hints

● Fresh herbs are used unless otherwise stated. If you are using dried herbs, reduce the quantities by half.

● Vegetable suet is used in a number of recipes. This is becoming widely available in supermarkets, but you could substitute beef suet if you cannot find the vegetable variety. The fat content is similar.

● Use freshly ground black pepper.

● Unless you are using a fan-assisted oven, always preheat the oven to the specified temperature.

BREAKFAST

Wholemeal bran loaf

Makes 2 loaves, 20 slices
Per slice: 118 kcal, 500 KJ, 4.4 g protein, 1.6 g fat, 23 g carbohydrate, 0.9 g soluble fibre, 2.4 g insoluble fibre

625 g/1 lb 6 oz wholewheat flour
50 g/2 oz oat bran and oat germ
10 ml/2 tsp salt
15 g/½ oz dried yeast
10 ml/2 tsp sugar
450 ml/¾ pint warm water
15 ml/1 tbsp sunflower oil
oat bran and oat germ, for sprinkling

Heat the oven to 220°C/425°F/gas 7.
   Mix the flour, oat bran and oat germ, and salt in a large bowl. Sprinkle the yeast and sugar over the water and stir to mix. Leave for about 10 minutes, until frothy. Add the yeast liquid and oil to the dry ingredients and mix to form a soft dough. Turn out on to a lightly floured surface and knead for 10 minutes, until the dough is smooth and pliable. Return the dough to the bowl and cover. Leave to rise for about 1 hour until the dough has doubled in size.
   Knead again briefly, then divide into two and place in two well greased 900 g/2 lb loaf tins. Sprinkle the loaves with oat bran and oat germ, cover and leave to rise again for about 45 minutes, until well risen.
   Bake for 35–45 minutes until the loaves are nicely browned and they sound hollow when tapped on the base. Cool on a wire rack.

Muesli bars

Makes 15 bars
Per bar: 162 kcal, 675 KJ, 2 g protein, 12.6 g fat,
10.9 g carbohydrate, 0.3 g soluble fibre, 0.6 g insoluble fibre

45 ml/3 tbsp honey
125 ml/4 fl oz sunflower oil
50 g/2 oz soft brown sugar
50 g/2 oz flaked almonds
100 g/4 oz rolled oats
25 g/1 oz desiccated coconut
25 g/1 oz sesame seeds

Heat the oven to 180°C/350°F/gas 4.
   In a mixing bowl mix the honey, oil and sugar. Stir in the almonds, rolled oats, coconut and sesame seeds. Spread over a greased 28 × 18 cm/11 × 7 inch shallow oblong tin.
   Bake for 20 minutes, until lightly browned. Cut into three down lengths and five across while still warm.

Breakfast roes

Serves 4
Per serving: 275 kcal, 1152 KJ, 31 g protein, 11.9 g fat,
11.6 g carbohydrate, 0.6 g soluble fibre, 0.6 g insoluble fibre

450 g/1 lb fresh cod's roe   *pepper*
1 bay leaf   *1 egg, beaten*
salt   *50 g/2 oz medium oatmeal*
15 ml/1 tbsp wholewheat flour   *30 ml/2 tbsp sunflower oil*

Place the roe in a pan with the bay leaf, a little salt and water to
cover. Bring to the boil, then cover and simmer for 15 minutes.
Remove with a slotted spoon and drain well on kitchen paper.
Place between two plates with a weight on top until cold.
   Cut the roe into thick slices and toss in flour. Sprinkle with
pepper. Coat in egg, then oatmeal until well covered.
   Heat the oil in a large pan, add the roes and fry on both sides
until golden brown, about 6–8 minutes. Drain on kitchen paper
and serve hot with lemon wedges.

Creamy raisin porridge

Serves 4
Per serving: 156 kcal, 662 KJ, 5.8 g protein, 2.25 g fat,
30 g carbohydrate, 1.2 g soluble fibre, 1 g insoluble fibre

300 ml/½ pint skimmed milk   *50 g/2 oz raisins*
600 ml/1 pint water   *100 g/4 oz Superfast oats*
2.5 ml/½ tsp ground cinnamon

Place the milk, water, cinnamon and raisins in a saucepan and
bring to the boil. Stir in the oats, then reduce the heat and simmer
for 4–5 minutes, until thick and creamy. Serve each bowl with a
swirl of low-fat natural yoghurt.

Oat bran and oat germ apple porridge

Serves 2
Per serving: 165 kcal, 700 KJ, 5.8 g protein, 3.4 g fat,
29.6 g carbohydrate, 1.7 g soluble fibre, 1.1 g insoluble fibre

150 ml/¼ pint apple juice
150 ml/¼ pint semi-skimmed milk
45 ml/3 tbsp oat bran and oat germ

Place all the ingredients in a small pan and bring to the boil, stirring all the time. Simmer for 3 minutes, until thickened and
smooth. Serve with a little honey and natural yoghurt.

Oatmeal bannocks

Makes 8
Per bannock: 161 kcal, 681 KJ, 4.3 g protein, 4.7 g fat,
27.1 g carbohydrate, 0.6 g soluble fibre, 0.5 g insoluble fibre

175 g/6 oz self-raising flour
100 g/4 oz fine oatmeal
5 ml/1 tsp bicarbonate of soda
2.5 ml/½ tsp cream of tartar

2.5 ml/½ tsp salt
25 g/1 oz polyunsaturated margarine
175 ml/6 fl oz milk

Heat the oven to 200°C/400°F/gas 6.

Mix together the flour, oatmeal, bicarbonate of soda, cream of
tartar and salt in a bowl. Rub in the margarine.

Stir in the milk all at once and quickly mix with a fork to form a
soft dough. Knead lightly on a floured surface, then roll out to a
round about 1 cm/½ inch thick and 20 cm/8 inches across. Cut
into eight wedges and place, a little apart, on a baking sheet. Bake
for 10–12 minutes, until lightly browned. Serve warm, split and
buttered with preserves or honey. Alternatively, these bannocks
can be cooked on a hot griddle for 10 minutes, turning once.

Herrings fried in oatmeal

Serves 4
Per serving: 167 kcal, 697 KJ, 13 g protein, 8.6 g fat,
10 g carbohydrate, 0.5 g soluble fibre, 0.4 g insoluble fibre

4 herrings, about 225 g/8 oz each
salt and pepper
30 ml/2 tbsp lemon juice

50 g/2 oz medium or coarse oatmeal
60 ml/4 tbsp sunflower or corn oil
parsley and lemon wedges, to garnish

Remove the heads from the herrings. Scrape off the scales with
the back of a knife and remove the guts. Wash the herrings
thoroughly. Spread the herrings out flat, skin side up. Press firmly
down the backbone, then turn them over and carefully lift out
the bones.

Dry the fish well with kitchen paper, then sprinkle the flesh
with a little salt, pepper and lemon juice. Coat each fish with oatmeal, pressing it firmly into the skin and flesh. If time allows, chill
the fish to set the coating.

Heat the oil in a large frying pan, large enough to take all the
fish. Add the herrings and fry gently for 10–12 minutes, turning
once, until tender. Drain on kitchen paper and serve piping hot
garnished with parsley and lemon wedges.

Fresh fruit muesli

Serves 4
Per serving: 136 kcal, 571 KJ, 4.8 g protein, 4.3 g fat,
20.8 g carbohydrate

150 ml/¼ pint natural low-fat yoghurt   *25 g/1 oz chopped hazelnuts*
60 ml/4 tbsp fresh orange juice   *100 g/4 oz apple, cored and chopped*
75 g/3 oz jumbo oats

Place all the ingredients in a bowl and mix well. Leave for 10
minutes before serving.

Variations Replace the apple with any of the following fruit in
season: 100 g/4 oz strawberries, sliced, 100 g/4 oz satsumas,
segmented, 100 g/4 oz cherries, stoned, 75 g/3 oz raspberries or
75 g/3 oz banana, sliced.

Jumbo oats granola

Serves 14
Per serving: 400 kcal, 1676 KJ, 8.4 g protein, 21.7 g fat,
42.5 g carbohydrate, 0.8 g soluble fibre, 1.2 g insoluble fibre

450 g/1 lb jumbo oats   *75 g/3 oz sunflower seeds*
50 g/2 oz oat bran and oat germ   *150 ml/¼ pint sunflower oil*
100 g/4 oz hazelnuts   *175 ml/6 fl oz clear honey*
50 g/2 oz raw peanuts   *100 g/4 oz sultanas*
75 g/3 oz sesame seeds

Heat the oven to 140°C/275°F/gas 1.
   Place the oats in a large bowl. Add the oat bran and oat germ,
hazelnuts, peanuts, sesame seeds and sunflower seeds, mixing
them together well. Pour in the oil gradually, mixing all the time,
then pour in the honey and stir until evenly mixed. Transfer the
mixture to a large roasting tin and spread out evenly.
   Bake for 1–1½ hours, stirring occasionally until slightly crispy.
Cool, then crumble up the mixture. Stir in the sultanas and
transfer to a stoppered jar.

Oatmeal muffins

Makes 10 See photograph, page 33
Per muffin: 116 kcal, 486 KJ, 2.6 g protein, 5.2 g fat,
15.5 g carbohydrate, 0.4 g soluble fibre, 0.9 g insoluble fibre

100 g/4 oz wholewheat flour *50 g/2 oz soft brown sugar*
2.5 ml/½ tsp baking powder *50 g/2 oz polyunsaturated margarine*
2.5 ml/½ tsp bicarbonate of soda *1 egg, beaten*
50 g/2 oz medium oatmeal *175 ml/6 fl oz buttermilk*

Heat the oven to 200°C/400°F/gas 6.
   Thoroughly mix the flour, baking powder, bicarbonate of soda, oatmeal and sugar in a bowl.
   Heat the margarine until just melted. Gently stir into the dry ingredients with the egg and buttermilk. Do not overmix. Place paper cake cases in bun tins and two-thirds fill with the mixture. Bake for 20–25 minutes until well risen and firm to the touch. Serve warm with cheese, jam or honey.

Ambrosia

Serves 4
Per serving: 96 kcal, 400 KJ, 1.2 g protein, 3.9 g fat,
14.7 g carbohydrate, 1.2 g soluble fibre, 0.7 g insoluble fibre

2 oranges, about 100 g/4 oz each *60 ml/4 tbsp pineapple juice*
100 g/4 oz strawberries, halved *25 g/1 oz rolled oats*
225 g/8 oz fresh pineapple, cubed *25 g/1 oz desiccated coconut*
pinch ground cinnamon

Grate 5 ml/1 tsp rind from one orange. Remove all the peel and white pith from the oranges. Cut down between the membranes to separate into segments. Place the orange segments, orange rind, strawberries, pineapple, cinnamon and pineapple juice in a bowl. Mix well.
   Spread the oats and coconut on a piece of foil and place under a moderate grill until lightly toasted. Cool, then sprinkle over the fruit.

Tropical muesli

Serves 10
Per serving: 383 kcal, 1611 KJ, 11.4 g protein, 15.4 g fat,
44.9 g carbohydrate, 3.2 g soluble fibre, 3 g insoluble fibre

450 g/1 lb jumbo oats
50 g/2 oz oat bran and oat germ
50 g/2 oz cashew nuts
100 g/4 oz raw peanuts

50 g/2 oz desiccated coconut
75 g/3 oz sunflower seeds
50 g/2 oz dried banana slices
75 g/3 oz dried peaches, chopped

Mix together all the ingredients until well blended. Store in a covered container for up to 3 weeks. Serve with natural yoghurt or skimmed milk. Add fresh fruit, too, when available, or squeeze over some fresh orange juice.

One minute porridge

Serves 4
Per serving: 263 kcal, 1111 KJ, 8.8 g protein, 7.1 g fat,
43.6 g carbohydrate, 2 g soluble fibre, 1.6 g insoluble fibre

475 ml/16 fl oz water, or milk and
  water mixed

pinch salt, optional
225 ml/8 fl oz Superfast oats

Place the liquid in a saucepan with the salt, if used, and heat until lukewarm. Stir in the oats, and bring to the boil. Simmer for 1 minute, stirring all the time, until the porridge is thickened and creamy. Serve the porridge with a sprinkling of sugar or salt or a little honey and milk.

Oatmeal porridge

Serves 4
Per serving: 99 kcal, 416 KJ, 4 g protein, 3.9 g fat,
12.6 g carbohydrate, 0.5 g soluble fibre, 0.4 g insoluble fibre

600 ml/1 pint water, or milk and
  water mixed

pinch salt, optional
50 g/2 oz medium oatmeal

Place the liquid in a saucepan with the salt, if used, and bring to the boil. Gradually sprinkle in the oatmeal, stirring well. Simmer, stirring all the time, for about 5 minutes, until the porridge has started to thicken, then simmer for a further 15–20 minutes, stirring occasionally, until the oatmeal is tender. Serve as for One Minute Porridge.

Tropical muesli (*above*); Oatmeal muffins (*below*, see page 31).

Sesame oat rolls

Makes 16
Per roll: 108 kcal, 455 KJ, 3.9 g protein, 3.5 g fat, 16.4 g carbohydrate,
0.7 g soluble fibre, 1.6 g insoluble fibre

275 g/10 oz wholewheat flour	*10 ml/2 tsp dried yeast*
100 g/4 oz rolled oats	*15 ml/1 tbsp sunflower oil*
50 g/2 oz sesame seeds	
5 ml/1 tsp salt	Topping:
300 ml/½ pint hand-hot water	*15 ml/1 tbsp milk*
5 ml/1 tsp sugar	*15 ml/1 tbsp rolled oats*
	10 ml/2 tsp sesame seeds

Mix the flour, oats, sesame seeds and salt in a bowl. Measure the
water into a jug and sprinkle over the sugar and yeast. Leave for
about 10 minutes, until frothy.

Add the yeast liquid and oil to the dry ingredients and mix to
form a soft dough. Knead for about 10 minutes, until smooth and
pliable. Divide into sixteen equal pieces and shape into rolls.
Place, well apart, on greased baking sheets. Cover with oiled
polythene and leave to rise for about 1 hour. Heat the oven to
220°C/425°F/gas 7.

Brush the rolls with milk and sprinkle with oats and sesame
seeds. Bake for 15–18 minutes, until risen and brown. Cool on a
wire rack.

Herbed haddock cakes

Serves 4
Per serving: 333 kcal, 1405 KJ, 30.6 g protein, 10.9 g fat,
30 g carbohydrate, 1.3 g soluble fibre, 0.9 g insoluble fibre

450 g/1 lb cooked haddock, skinned,	*pinch cayenne pepper*
boned and flaked	*salt*
450 g/1 lb cooked potatoes, mashed	*2.5 ml/½ tsp grated lemon rind*
5 ml/1 tsp chopped tarragon	*1 egg, beaten*
5 ml/1 tsp chopped dill	*50 g/2 oz medium oatmeal*
15 ml/1 tbsp snipped chives	*30 ml/2 tbsp sunflower oil*

Mix the fish with the potatoes, herbs, pepper, salt and lemon rind.
Form into eight flat cakes, then brush with egg and coat in oatmeal. Chill for 30 minutes. Heat the oil in a large pan, add the fish
cakes and fry for 10 minutes on each side, until crisp and
golden.

Herbed haddock cakes (*above*); Sesame oat rolls (*below*).

SOUPS, FIRST COURSES AND SNACKS

Ham and oatmeal broth

Serves 6
Per serving: 327 kcal, 1363 KJ, 18.5 g protein, 21 g fat, 16 g carbohydrate, 2.4 g soluble fibre, 2 g insoluble fibre

450 g/1 lb bacon knuckle, soaked
  overnight
175 g/6 oz onions, chopped
175 g/6 oz carrots, chopped
100 g/4 oz parsnips, chopped
100 g/4 oz swede, diced

bouquet garni
75 g/3 oz leek, sliced
75 g/3 oz medium oatmeal
100 g/4 oz green cabbage, shredded
pepper
30 ml/2 tbsp chopped parsley

Place the bacon in a large pan with 1.8 litres/3 pints water. Add the onions, carrots, parsnips, swede and bouquet garni and bring to the boil. Cover and simmer for 30 minutes. Stir in the leek, oatmeal and cabbage and simmer for 30 minutes more, stirring occasionally. Remove the bacon and strip the meat from the bone, discarding the skin and fat. Dice the meat and add to the soup with pepper and parsley. Simmer for 10 minutes.

Watercress and lemon soup

Serves 4   See photograph, page 51
Per serving: 110 kcal, 459 KJ, 2.8 g protein, 6.4 g fat, 10.7 g carbohydrate, 1.3 g soluble fibre, 1 g insoluble fibre

25 g/1 oz polyunsaturated margarine
50 g/2 oz celery, finely chopped
50 g/2 oz onion, finely chopped
5 ml/1 tsp grated lemon rind
600 ml/1 pint vegetable stock

600 ml/1 pint semi-skimmed milk
50 g/2 oz oat bran and oat germ
75 g/3 oz watercress, finely chopped
pepper

Melt the margarine in a large pan, add the celery and onion and fry until softened, about 5 minutes. Add the lemon rind, stock and milk and bring to the boil. Simmer for 5 minutes. Sprinkle over the oat bran and oat germ then stir in with the watercress and pepper, and simmer for a further 5 minutes, until thickened.

Oat and lentil soup

Serves 6
Per serving: 137 kcal, 580 KJ, 6.4 g protein, 4.6 g fat,
18.8 g carbohydrate, 1.1 g soluble fibre, 1 g insoluble fibre

25 g/1 oz polyunsaturated margarine
175 g/6 oz onions, chopped
1 clove garlic, crushed
100 g/4 oz red lentils
100 g/4 oz carrots, chopped
100 g/4 oz celery, chopped

900 ml/1½ pint vegetable stock
10 ml/2 tsp soy sauce
50 g/2 oz fine oatmeal
pepper
150 ml/¼ pint semi-skimmed milk

Melt the margarine in a large saucepan, add the onions and garlic and cook until softened, about 5 minutes. Add the lentils, carrots and celery and stir well. Add the stock and soy sauce and bring to the boil. Stir in the oatmeal in a steady stream and cook until thickened. Add plenty of pepper, cover and simmer for 25 minutes, until the vegetables are tender. Stir in the milk and heat through gently. Serve with granary rolls.

Carrot and orange soup

Serves 4
Per serving: 150 kcal, 629 KJ, 3.8 g protein, 7.6 g fat,
17.8 g carbohydrate, 1.6 g soluble fibre, 1.2 g insoluble fibre

25 g/1 oz polyunsaturated margarine
325 g/12 oz carrots, chopped
175 g/6 oz onion, chopped
50 g/2 oz fine oatmeal
900 ml/1½ pints vegetable stock

5 ml/1 tsp grated orange rind
60 ml/4 tbsp orange juice
pepper
150 ml/¼ pint milk
salt, optional

Melt the margarine in a large pan, add the carrots and onion and stir well. Add the oatmeal and cook for 1 minute. Gradually stir in the stock and bring to the boil.
Cover and simmer for 20 minutes, until the vegetables are tender. Purée the soup in a blender or food processor, then return to the pan and add the orange rind, juice, pepper and milk. Reheat gently and add salt if necessary.

Oatmeal dumplings

Makes 8
Per dumpling: 97 kcal, 403 KJ, 1.6 g protein, 6 g fat,
9.4 g carbohydrate, 0.3 g soluble fibre, 0.6 g insoluble fibre

50 g/2 oz self-raising wholewheat   *50 g/2 oz vegetable suet*
   flour   *pinch salt*
50 g/2 oz medium oatmeal

Mix together the flour, oatmeal, suet and salt. Add cold water to
form a soft dough. Shape into eight balls and add to soups and
stews for the last 20–30 minutes of the cooking time. Cover the
pan while the dumplings are cooking.

Variations For Onion Dumplings add 50 g/2 oz finely chopped
onion to the dry mix. For Caraway Dumplings add 5 ml/1 tsp
caraway seeds to the dry mix. For Parsley and Lemon Dumplings
add 30 ml/2 tbsp chopped parsley and 2.5 ml/½ tsp grated lemon
rind to the dry mix. For Horseradish Dumplings add 25 g/1 oz
grated horseradish to the dry mix.

Oatmeal vegetable soup

Serves 6
Per serving: 146 kcal, 615 KJ, 3.4 g protein, 6.1 g fat,
20.7 g carbohydrate, 1.6 g soluble fibre, 1.4 g insoluble fibre

30 ml/2 tbsp sunflower oil   *75 g/3 oz medium oatmeal*
2 medium onions, chopped   *225 g/8 oz can tomatoes*
2 sticks celery, chopped   *15 ml/1 tbsp concentrated vegetable*
225 g/8 oz potatoes, peeled and   *stock*
   chopped   *1.5 litres/2½ pints water*
2 medium carrots, chopped   *salt and pepper*

Heat the oil in a large saucepan. Add the vegetables and stir in the
oil until evenly coated. Add the oatmeal and cook for 5
minutes.
   Add the tomatoes, stock and water and bring to the boil. Partially cover and simmer for 25–30 minutes until the vegetables are
tender. Place half the soup in a blender or food processor and
blend until smooth. Return to the pan and reheat. Taste and add
salt and pepper.
   To serve, sprinkle with grated cheese, or drop in small
pieces of mozzarella.

Oatmeal and onion soup

Serves 4
Per serving: 287 kcal, 1198 KJ, 10.3 g protein, 18.8 g fat,
20.4 g carbohydrate, 1.5 g soluble fibre, 1.7 g insoluble fibre

25 g/1 oz butter or polyunsaturated margarine
15 ml/1 tbsp oil
2 medium onions, chopped
50 g/2 oz medium oatmeal

1.2 litres/2 pints canned beef consommé or rich vegetable stock
5 ml/1 tsp Dijon mustard
salt and pepper
4 slices wholewheat bread
100 g/4 oz Cheddar cheese, grated

Heat the fat and oil in a saucepan, add the onions and fry gently for 15 minutes, until lightly browned, stirring frequently. Add the oatmeal and fry for 5 minutes. Stir in the consommé or stock gradually, then bring to the boil. Add the mustard and simmer, partly covered, for 30 minutes. Taste and add salt, if necessary, and pepper.

Divide the soup between four heatproof bowls. Cut each bread slice into four and float on each bowl of soup. Sprinkle with cheese and place under a hot grill until the cheese is melted and lightly browned.

Cheese and leek soup

Serves 4
Per serving: 215 kcal, 897 KJ, 9.2 g protein, 13.1 g fat,
15.8 g carbohydrate, 1.5 g soluble fibre, 1.3 g insoluble fibre

25 g/1 oz butter or polyunsaturated margarine
325 g/12 oz leeks, finely shredded
50 g/2 oz fine oatmeal
600 ml/1 pint vegetable stock

150 ml/¼ pint semi-skimmed milk
75 g/3 oz Lancashire cheese, crumbled
salt and pepper
15 ml/1 tbsp chopped parsley

Melt the butter or margarine in a saucepan, add the leeks and cook gently until softened. Stir in the oatmeal and cook for 1 minute. Add the stock and bring to the boil. Cover and simmer for 20 minutes.

Liquidize until smooth, then return to the saucepan. Stir in the milk, cheese, salt and pepper. Reheat gently, stirring until the cheese has melted. Add the parsley just before serving.

Cheshire soup

Serves 4
Per serving: 169 kcal, 712 KJ, 7 g protein, 5.3 g fat,
24.8 g carbohydrate, 1.7 g soluble fibre, 1.4 g insoluble fibre

1.2 litres/2 pints vegetable stock
225 g/8 oz potatoes, peeled and diced
175 g/6 oz leeks, chopped
pepper
100 g/4 oz carrots, grated
50 g/2 oz medium oatmeal
50 g/2 oz Cheshire cheese, grated

Place the stock in a large saucepan with the potatoes, leeks and pepper. Bring to the boil, then simmer for 15 minutes. Add the carrots and whisk in the oatmeal. Simmer for a further 15–20 minutes until the oatmeal is tender. Remove from the heat and stir in the cheese.

Camembert in an oat crust

Serves 4 as a starter   See photograph, page 51
Per serving: 287 kcal, 1193 KJ, 14.5 g protein, 21 g fat,
10.7 g carbohydrate, 1.2 g soluble fibre, 0.9 g insoluble fibre

225 g/8 oz whole Camembert
1 egg, beaten
50 g/2 oz medium oatmeal, toasted
4 large lettuce leaves
100 g/4 oz strawberries
1 large orange, about 175 g/6 oz
15 g/½ oz butter or polyunsaturated margarine
15 ml/1 tbsp sunflower oil

Cut the Camembert into quarters. Toss each piece in egg, then coat in some oatmeal. Repeat the process until the cheese is well coated. Chill for 30 minutes.

Arrange a lettuce leaf on each serving plate. Slice the strawberries. Peel and segment the orange. Divide the fruit between the plates.

Heat the fat and oil in a small frying pan. Add the cheese pieces and fry on all sides until evenly browned, about 5 minutes. Drain on kitchen paper, place on the serving plates and serve at once.

Mushroom pâté

Serves 6
Per serving: 116 kcal, 485 KJ, 5.3 g protein, 5.6 g fat,
10.3 g carbohydrate, 0.8 g soluble fibre, 1.2 g insoluble fibre

25 g/1 oz polyunsaturated margarine
100 g/4 oz onion, finely chopped
450 g/1 lb cup or open mushrooms,
  finely chopped
75 g/3 oz rolled oats
150 ml/¼ pint vegetable stock
30 ml/2 tbsp sherry or madeira,
  optional
salt and pepper
100 g/4 oz low-fat soft cheese
2 slices lemon

Melt the margarine in a saucepan, add the onion and cook until softened, about 5 minutes. Add the mushrooms and cook for 2 minutes, stirring all the time. Add the oats, stock, sherry or madeira, if used, a little salt and plenty of pepper. Cook over a very low heat for 5 minutes, stirring all the time. Remove from the heat and stir in the soft cheese, mixing well. Press into a dish and leave to cool, then chill until firm. Garnish with lemon slices.

Smoked mackerel pâté

Serves 4
Per serving: 257 kcal, 1073 KJ, 20.5 g protein, 15.3 g fat,
9.8 g carbohydrate, 0.5 g soluble fibre, 0.4 g insoluble fibre

325 g/12 oz smoked mackerel fillets
100 g/4 oz low-fat soft cheese
50 g/2 oz Toasted Oats, see page
  49
10 ml/2 tsp horseradish sauce
15 ml/1 tbsp lemon juice
pepper

Skin the mackerel, then flake the fish finely into a bowl. Beat in the cheese until fairly smooth, then add the oats, horseradish, lemon juice and pepper. Press into a bowl and chill until firm. Serve with toast or crackers, or in sandwiches.

Pissaladière

Serves 8   See photograph, page 52
Per serving: 226 kcal, 943 KJ, 5.4 g protein, 14.8 g fat,
18.9 g carbohydrate, 1.5 g soluble fibre, 2.2 g insoluble fibre

1 quantity High Fibre Pastry, see   salt and pepper
*   page 120   325 g/12 oz tomatoes, sliced*
30 ml/2 tbsp sunflower oil   50 g/2 oz Cheddar cheese, grated
450 g/1 lb onions, thinly sliced   50 g/2 oz black olives
2 cloves garlic, crushed

Heat the oven to 200°C/400°F/gas 6.
Roll out the pastry and line a 23 × 33 cm/9 × 13 inch shallow oblong tin. Chill while you make the filling.
Heat the oil in a frying pan, add the onions and garlic and fry for about 10 minutes, until the onions are softened and lightly browned. Season with a little salt and pepper. Cool.
Spread the onion mixture over the pastry case, arrange the tomato slices over the top and sprinkle with cheese. Place the olives on top. Bake for 35 minutes, until the topping is bubbling and the pastry crisp and golden. Serve warm or cold, cut into slices.

Stuffed peppers

Serves 4
Per serving: 273 kcal, 1144 KJ, 11.1 g protein, 17 g fat,
20.5 g carbohydrate, 2.6 g soluble fibre, 2.9 g insoluble fibre

4 green or red peppers, about   5 ml/1 tsp mixed herbs
*   150 g/5 oz each   50 g/2 oz stuffed olives, sliced*
30 ml/2 tbsp olive oil   175 g/6 oz tomatoes, chopped
175 g/6 oz onion, chopped   75 g/3 oz rolled oats
1 clove garlic, crushed   100 g/4 oz Edam cheese, grated
100 g/4 oz button mushrooms, sliced

Heat the oven to 190°C/375°F/gas 5.
Cut the peppers in half through the stalk and remove the seeds. Blanch in boiling water for 2 minutes, then drain well.
Heat the oil in a pan, add the onion and garlic and fry for 5 minutes, until softened. Add the mushrooms, herbs, olives, tomatoes and oats and mix well. Remove from the heat and stir in half the cheese. Place the peppers in a roasting tin and stuff with the oat mixture. Sprinkle with the remaining cheese. Bake, uncovered, for 30 minutes.

Cheese-stuffed tomatoes

Serves 4
Per serving: 222 kcal, 925 KJ, 9.6 g protein, 14.5 g fat,
14 g carbohydrate, 1.5 g soluble fibre, 1.8 g insoluble fibre

4 beefsteak tomatoes, about
  175 g/6 oz each
salt
50 g/2 oz rolled oats
100 g/4 oz mature Cheddar cheese,
  grated

1 clove garlic, crushed
pepper
25 g/1 oz butter or polyunsaturated
  margarine

Heat the oven to 190°C/375°F/gas 5.

Cut the tomatoes in halves and scoop out the flesh. Chop the flesh and reserve. Sprinkle them inside with a little salt and place upside down on kitchen paper to drain.

Spread the oats over a baking tray and bake for 10 minutes, until toasted. Cool slightly, then mix with the cheese, garlic, tomato flesh and pepper. Pile into the tomato shells, pressing down lightly. Place a small knob of butter or margarine on top of each.

Place the tomatoes in an oiled baking dish and bake for 25–30 minutes, until the tomatoes are tender and the filling is crisp on top. Serve warm.

Stuffed mushrooms

Serves 4
Per serving: 149 kcal, 620 KJ, 8.9 g protein, 8.7 g fat,
9.1 g carbohydrate, 0.6 g soluble fibre, 0.9 g insoluble fibre

4 large open mushrooms, about
  50 g/2 oz each
75 g/3 oz lean bacon, chopped
50 g/2 oz rolled oats
1 clove garlic, crushed

15 ml/1 tbsp chopped parsley
pepper
30 ml/2 tbsp grated Parmesan cheese
15 ml/1 tbsp sunflower oil

Heat the oven to 200°C/400°F/gas 6.

Remove the stalks from the mushrooms and chop the stalks finely. Place the mushrooms in an oiled ovenproof dish. Mix the mushroom stalks with the bacon, oats, garlic, parsley, pepper, cheese and oil. Pile on to the mushrooms, then cover with foil and bake for 10 minutes. Remove the foil and bake for a further 5 minutes to crisp the tops.

Stuffed potatoes

Serves 4
Per serving: 350 kcal, 1480 KJ, 14.6 g protein, 8.4 g fat,
57 g carbohydrate, 2.2 g soluble fibre, 1.7 g insoluble fibre

4 large baking potatoes, about
   225 g/8 oz each
100 g/4 oz Edam cheese, diced
50 g/2 oz medium oatmeal
10 ml/2 tsp paprika

1 egg, beaten
45 ml/3 tbsp natural low-fat yoghurt
salt and pepper
100 g/4 oz tomatoes, sliced

Heat the oven to 200°C/400°F/gas 6.

Prick the potatoes with a fork, then bake for about 1 hour, until tender. Cool slightly, cut in halves, and scoop the centres out into a bowl. Mash until smooth, then stir in the cheese, oatmeal, paprika, egg, yoghurt, salt and pepper. Pile the mixture back into the potato shells and top with sliced tomato. Return to the oven for 15–20 minutes, until the cheese has melted.

Vegetable loaf

Serves 6
Per serving: 210 kcal, 881 KJ, 9 g protein, 11.4 g fat,
18.8 g carbohydrate, 2.5 g soluble fibre, 2.6 g insoluble fibre

225 g/8 oz French beans
1 onion, grated
325 g/12 oz courgettes, grated
175 g/6 oz carrots, grated
75 g/3 oz hazelnuts, chopped
50 g/2 oz sunflower seeds

10 ml/2 tsp soy sauce
150 ml/¼ pint curd cheese
2 eggs, beaten
100 g/4 oz coarse oatmeal
salt and pepper

Heat the oven to 190°C/375°F/gas 5.

Chop the beans into 2.5 cm/1 inch lengths. Steam or boil for 5 minutes, then drain and cool quickly under running cold water. Mix with the onion, courgettes and carrots. Add the nuts, sunflower seeds, soy sauce, cheese and eggs, mixing well. Stir in the oatmeal and add a little salt and lots of pepper. Press into an oiled 1.2 1/2 pint loaf tin and smooth the top. Bake for 1 hour until firm to the touch.

Turn out and serve warm cut into thick slices.

Cheese log

Serves 10
Per serving: 333 kcal, 1383 KJ, 16.9 g protein, 25.4 g fat,
9.5 g carbohydrate, 0.5 g soluble fibre, 0.4 g insoluble fibre

100 g/4 oz medium oatmeal
225 g/8 oz curd cheese
450 g/1 lb mature Cheddar cheese,
  finely grated
100 g/4 oz packet soft cheese with
  herbs and garlic

15 ml/1 tbsp mayonnaise
10 ml/2 tsp soy sauce
2.5 ml/½ tsp cayenne pepper
25 g/1 oz walnuts, finely chopped
10 ml/2 tsp paprika

Spread the oatmeal over a baking sheet and place under a grill for
2–3 minutes until lightly toasted.

Beat together the cheeses and mayonnaise. Beat in the soy
sauce, cayenne, nuts and half the toasted oatmeal. Shape the mixture into a rough roll with damp hands, then place on a sheet of
foil and roll in the foil to obtain a neat log shape. Chill for 1
hour.

Mix the remaining oatmeal with the paprika. Unwrap the log
and roll in the oatmeal until evenly coated. Chill until you are
ready to serve it.

To serve, place on a bed of salad leaves, radishes and raw
mushroom slices. Cut into thin slices and serve with oatcakes,
crackers or bread.

Oatcakes

Makes 8
Per oatcake: 56 kcal, 235 KJ, 1.5 g protein, 1.7 g fat,
9.1 g carbohydrate, 0.5 g soluble fibre, 0.4 g insoluble fibre

100 g/4 oz fine oatmeal
pinch of salt
pinch of bicarbonate of soda

5 ml/1 tsp sunflower oil or bacon fat
60 ml/4 tbsp hot water

Mix together the oatmeal, salt and bicarbonate of soda. Add the
oil or fat and stir in the water until a stiff paste is formed. Knead
the mixture until smooth on a board sprinkled with oatmeal.

Press out to a rough circle, then roll out as thinly as possible to a
round about 23 cm/9 inches across. Cut into eight wedges. Cook
on one side only on a moderately hot griddle until the edges begin
to curl and the underside is dry. Toast the other side under a
moderate grill or place in a moderate oven until dried out.

Cool on a wire rack, then store in an airtight container.

Cheese and celery seed cob

Makes 1 large loaf, 12 slices
Per slice: 211 kcal, 889 KJ, 8.4 g protein, 7.4 g fat,
29.3 g carbohydrate, 1.2 g soluble fibre, 2.7 insoluble fibre

30 ml/2 tbsp sunflower oil
1 medium onion, finely chopped
300 ml/½ pint warm water
5 ml/1 tsp honey
10 ml/2 tsp dried yeast
400 g/14 oz wholewheat flour
100 g/4 oz medium oatmeal
5 ml/1 tsp salt
10 ml/2 tsp Dijon mustard
10 ml/2 tsp celery seeds
125 g/5 oz strong Cheddar cheese,
  finely grated
10 ml/2 tsp oatmeal, for sprinkling

Heat the oil in a small pan, add the onion and fry for about 5 minutes until lightly browned. Mix the water and honey, sprinkle over the yeast and leave until frothy, about 10 minutes.

Mix together the flour, oatmeal, salt, mustard, celery seeds and 100 g/4 oz of cheese. Add the onions with the oil and mix well. Add the yeast liquid and mix to a soft dough. Place on a floured surface and knead for 5 minutes until all the ingredients are well distributed.

Shape the dough into a round and place on a well-greased baking sheet. Cut a deep cross in the top. Cover with oiled polythene and leave to rise for 40–50 minutes until the dough is well risen and springs back when pressed.

Heat the oven to 220°C/425°F/gas 7.

Sprinkle the remaining cheese and a little oatmeal over the loaf and bake for 30–40 minutes until golden brown and the loaf sounds hollow when tapped on the base.

Vegetable oatcakes

Serves 4
Per serving: 306 kcal, 1276 KJ, 5.1 g protein, 22.8 g fat,
17.8 g carbohydrate, 1.9 g soluble fibre, 1.3 g insoluble fibre

1 medium onion, grated
1 medium carrot, grated
1 stick celery, finely chopped
60 ml/4 tbsp sunflower oil
50 g/2 oz oat bran and oat germ
50 g/2 oz rolled oats
50 g/2 oz mature Cheddar cheese,
  grated
1 egg, beaten
30 ml/2 tbsp milk
salt and pepper

Fry the vegetables in half the oil until softened, about 5 minutes. Mix three-quarters of the oat bran and oat germ with the rolled oats, add the fried vegetables, grated cheese, egg, milk and seasoning. Mix to a soft consistency and shape into eight round cakes. Coat them with the remaining oat bran and oat germ and fry in the remaining oil for 10 minutes until golden brown, turning once. Serve hot with vegetables or salad.

Crunchy cheese biscuits

Makes 24 biscuits
Per biscuit: 92 g kcal, 385 g KJ, 2.9 g protein, 6.4 g fat,
6.1 g carbohydrate, 0.3 g soluble fibre, 0.5 g insoluble fibre

*75 g/3 oz mature Cheddar, finely
  grated
25 g/1 oz Parmesan cheese, finely
  grated
100 g/4 oz wholewheat flour
100 g/4 oz rolled oats*

*5 ml/1 tsp dry mustard
100 g/4 oz polyunsaturated margarine,
  melted
45 ml/3 tbsp crunchy peanut butter
1 egg, beaten
15 ml/1 tbsp milk*

Heat the oven to 190°C/375°F/gas 5.

Mix together the cheeses, flour, oats and mustard in a bowl. Add the margarine, peanut butter, egg and milk and mix to a soft dough.

Sprinkle a surface with oatmeal and turn out the dough. Shape it into a roll about 5 cm/2 inches across and 20–25 cm/8–10 inches long. Wrap in foil and chill for 2 hours or longer until firm.

Using a large sharp knife cut thin slices from the roll and place them, a little apart, on greased baking sheets. Bake for 18–20 minutes until light golden. Cool on the baking sheets for 2 minutes, then cool on a wire rack. Store in a tin.

Crunchy cheese fries

Serves 8
Per serving: 148 kcal, 615 KJ, 8.4 g protein, 10.8 g fat,
4.6 g carbohydrate, 0.2 g soluble fibre, 0.2 g insoluble fibre

*225 g/8 oz Gruyère cheese
1 egg
30 ml/2 tbsp water*

*50 g/2 oz medium oatmeal
sea salt
oil, for deep frying*

Cut the cheese into 1 cm/½ inch cubes. Beat together the egg and water on a plate. Spread the oatmeal and a little sea salt on a second plate. Coat the cheese cubes in egg, then oatmeal and salt. Chill for 15 minutes, then coat again.

Heat the oil to 180°C/350°F. Add the cheese cubes and fry for about 5 minutes until the coating is crisp and golden brown. Drain well on kitchen paper, then serve hot on cocktail sticks with a spicy tomato sauce or béarnaise sauce for dipping.

Tuna and sweetcorn flan

Serves 6
Per serving: 309 kcal, 1292 KJ, 13.1 g protein, 19.1 g fat,
22.5 g carbohydrate, 1 g soluble fibre, 2 g insoluble fibre

1 quantity High Fibre Pastry, see
  page 120
198 g/7 oz can tuna in brine, drained
75 g/3 oz cooked sweetcorn
4 spring onions, chopped

2 eggs, beaten
300 ml/½ pint semi-skimmed milk
15 g/½ oz finely grated lemon rind
salt and pepper

Heat the oven to 200°C/400°F/gas 6.
   Roll out the pastry and line a 20–23 cm/8–9 inch flan tin. Prick
the base and bake blind for 10 minutes.
   Reduce the oven temperature to 180°C/350°F/gas 4. Flake the
tuna and arrange evenly over the flan case with the sweetcorn and
spring onions. Beat together the eggs, milk, lemon rind, salt and
pepper. Pour into the flan case and bake for 30–35 minutes until
the filling is set and golden brown. Serve warm or cold.

Cheese and oat scone round

Serves 8
Per serving: 211 kcal, 882 KJ, 8 g protein, 11 g fat,
21.1 g carbohydrate, 0.7 g soluble fibre, 1.9 g insoluble fibre

175 g/6 oz self-raising wholewheat
  flour
50 g/2 oz medium oatmeal
5 ml/1 tsp baking powder
50 g/2 oz polyunsaturated margarine
100 g/4 oz mature Cheddar cheese,
  grated

175 g/6 oz cooking apple, grated
1 egg, beaten
30 ml/2 tbsp milk
10 ml/2 tsp Dijon mustard
milk, to glaze
oats, to sprinkle

Heat the oven to 200°C/400°F/gas 6.
   Place the flour, oatmeal and baking powder in a bowl and mix
well. Add the margarine, in small pieces and rub in until the mixture resembles breadcrumbs. Stir in the cheese and apple and mix
thoroughly. Beat together the egg, milk and mustard and stir into
the dry ingredients to form a soft dough. Turn out on to a floured
surface and knead lightly.
   Shape into a round about 2.5 cm/1 inch thick and place on a
greased baking sheet. Mark into eight wedges with a sharp knife.
Brush with a little milk and sprinkle with oats. Bake for 25–30
minutes until risen and golden brown. Cool on a wire rack and
break into sections to serve.

Onion oat bread

Makes 1 loaf, serves 8
Per serving: 240 kcal, 1016 KJ, 8.8 g protein, 6.4 g fat,
39.2 g carbohydrate, 1.7 g soluble fibre, 4 g insoluble fibre

175 g/6 oz onions, peeled
2 tbsp sunflower oil
5 ml/1 tsp sugar
10 ml/2 tsp dried yeast
300 ml/½ pint warm water
400 g/14 oz wholewheat flour

50 g/2 oz rolled oats
10 ml/2 tsp celery seeds
5 ml/1 tsp salt
15 ml/1 tbsp dry mustard
30 ml/2 tbsp Parmesan cheese, grated

Cut the onions in half through root, then cut down into very thin slices. Heat the oil in a pan, add the onion and fry until soft and lightly browned. Reserve a few onion slices for the top.

Sprinkle the sugar and yeast over the water and leave for about 10 minutes, until frothy.

Mix together the flour, oats, celery seeds, salt and mustard. Make a well in the centre and add the yeast liquid and the onion slices with the oil they were cooked in. Mix to form a soft dough. Turn out on to a floured surface and knead for about 5 minutes, until smooth and pliable. Place in an oiled polythene bag and leave to rise for about 1 hour until doubled in size. Knead again briefly, then divide the dough in half. Shape each piece into a 25 cm/10 inch rope and twist the two pieces together, pinching the ends to seal. Place on a greased baking sheet. Brush with water, then sprinkle with the reserved onion and cheese. Cover again and leave for about 40 minutes until well risen.

Heat the oven to 220°C/425°F/gas 7. Bake the bread for 35–40 minutes until risen and well browned. The cooked loaf will sound hollow when tapped on the base. Cool on a wire rack and serve with soups or any main meals.

Toasted oats

Per quantity: 902 kcal, 3820 KJ, 27.9 g protein, 19.6 g fat, 163.8 g carbohydrate, 8.3 g soluble fibre, 6.5 g insoluble fibre

Sprinkle these over soups, desserts and salads. Use them in main meals for added crunch and texture. Use for coating patties and rissoles and in toppings in place of breadcrumbs.

Spread 225 g/8 oz rolled oats or jumbo oats over a baking sheet or roasting tin. Place in the oven at 180°C/350°F/gas 4 for 20–25 minutes, stirring them halfway through the cooking time.

Cool the oats, then store them in a stoppered jar for 3–4 weeks.

Spinach salad

Serves 4
Per serving: 237 kcal, 987 KJ, 6.6 g protein, 17.8 g fat,
13.3 g carbohydrate, 1.4 g soluble fibre, 1.7 g insoluble fibre

225 g/8 oz young spinach leaves
100 g/4 oz button mushrooms, sliced
1 egg, hard boiled and chopped
1 red eating apple, chopped
50 g/2 oz radishes, sliced

60 ml/4 tbsp sunflower oil
5 ml/1 tsp Dijon mustard
30 ml/2 tbsp lemon juice
pepper
50 g/2 oz Toasted Oats, see page 49

Wash the spinach thoroughly and dry well. Tear the leaves into large pieces and place in a salad bowl. Sprinkle over the mushrooms, egg, apple and radishes.

Whisk together the oil, mustard, lemon juice and pepper. Pour over the salad and toss thoroughly. Sprinkle with oats and serve immediately.

Crunchy salad

Serves 4　　　　　　　　　　See photograph, page 62
Per serving: 259 kcal, 1082 KJ, 4.7 g protein, 17 g fat,
23.5 g carbohydrate, 2.2 g soluble fibre, 2.2 g insoluble fibre

225 g/8 oz white cabbage, finely
*　shredded*
100 g/4 oz carrots, grated
100 g/4 oz celery, chopped
50 g/2 oz raisins
50 g/2 oz hazelnuts, chopped

50 g/2 oz Toasted Oats, see page 49
45 ml/3 tbsp sunflower oil
15 ml/1 tbsp lemon juice
5 ml/1 tsp clear honey
45 ml/3 tbsp natural low-fat yoghurt
pepper

Mix the vegetables with the raisins, nuts and oats. Whisk together the remaining ingredients until smooth and pour over the salad, mixing it well.

Camembert in an oat crust (*top*, see page 40); Spinach salad (*centre*); Watercress and lemon soup (*bottom*, see page 36).

Liver and orange pâté

Serves 6
**Per serving: 177 kcal, 742 KJ, 16.1 g protein, 8.9 g fat,
8.7 g carbohydrate, 0.5 g soluble fibre, 0.4 g insoluble fibre**

450 g/1 lb chicken livers
25 g/1 oz polyunsaturated margarine
100 g/4 oz onion, chopped
1 clove garlic, crushed
45 ml/3 tbsp orange juice
5 ml/1 tsp finely grated orange rind
45 ml/3 tbsp sherry or stock

50 g/2 oz fine oatmeal
pepper
60 ml/4 tbsp set low-fat yoghurt
bay leaves and orange slices, to garnish
15 g/½ oz polyunsaturated margarine,
*   melted (optional)*

Trim off any dark patches from the livers. Rinse and pat dry with kitchen paper. Melt 25 g/1 oz margarine in a saucepan, add the onion and garlic and fry until softened, about 5 minutes. Add the chicken livers and fry until browned on all sides. Add the orange juice, rind, sherry or stock and oatmeal and cook, covered, for 5 minutes.

Place the mixture in a blender or food processor with a good shake of pepper and the yoghurt. Purée until fairly smooth. Press the pâté into a dish and smooth the top. Garnish with bay leaves and orange slices. Pour over 15 g/½ oz melted margarine, if using. Cover and store in the fridge for up to 2 days.

Pissaladière (*above*, see page 42); Liver and orange pâté (*below*).

VEGETARIAN DISHES

Aubergine and tomato bake

Serves 4
Per serving: 602 kcal, 2523 KJ, 36.6 g protein, 32.1 g fat,
44.5 g carbohydrate, 2.1 g soluble fibre, 1.9 g insoluble fibre

450 g/1 lb aubergines
1 egg, beaten
100 g/4 oz medium oatmeal
45 ml/3 tbsp olive oil
2 × 400 g/14 oz cans passata (puréed tomatoes, available from large supermarkets)

2 cloves garlic, crushed
5 ml/1 tsp oregano
pepper
225 g/8 oz mozzarella cheese
60 ml/4 tbsp grated Parmesan cheese

Heat the oven to 190°C/375°F/gas 5.

Cut the aubergines into thin slices. Dip in egg, then coat in the oatmeal, pressing it on firmly. Heat the oil in a large frying pan, add the aubergines and fry on both sides until lightly browned, about 5 minutes. Drain on kitchen paper.

Mix together the passata, garlic, oregano and pepper. Slice the mozzarella thinly. Arrange the aubergines over the base of a shallow ovenproof dish. Place the mozzarella slices on top. Pour over the tomato sauce and sprinkle with Parmesan.

Bake for 30–35 minutes, until the cheese is melted and the topping is lightly browned. Serve hot with a green salad and hot garlic bread.

Summer stir-fry

Serves 4   See photograph, page 61
Per serving: 168 kcal, 708 KJ, 5.1 g protein, 6.1 g fat,
24.6 carbohydrate, 2.4 g soluble fibre, 2.5 g insoluble fibre

15 ml/1 tbsp sunflower oil
175 g/6 oz onion, thinly sliced
1 clove garlic, crushed
100 g/4 oz green pepper, seeded and
  sliced
100 g/4 oz courgettes, sliced
50 g/2 oz mushrooms, sliced
100 g/4 oz rolled oats
450 g/1 lb tomatoes, chopped
salt and pepper

Heat the oil in a large frying pan. Add the onion and garlic and cook, stirring, over a high heat until just softened, about 2 minutes. Add the peppers, courgettes and mushrooms and cook for 2 minutes more. Stir in the oats and cook for 1 minute, stirring all the time. Add the tomatoes, a little salt and a good shake of pepper. Simmer for 3 minutes, stirring all the time. Serve piping hot.

Oatmeal and watercress soufflé

Serves 4
Per serving: 259 kcal, 1085 KJ, 13.7 g protein, 15.6 g fat,
17 g carbohydrate, 1 g soluble fibre, 0.8 g insoluble fibre

25 g/1 oz polyunsaturated margarine
100 g/4 oz onion, chopped
75 g/3 oz medium oatmeal
150 ml/¼ pint vegetable stock
150 ml/¼ pint semi-skimmed milk
100 g/4 oz watercress, finely chopped
100 g/4 oz Edam cheese, diced
2 eggs, separated
10 ml/2 tsp Dijon mustard
pepper
15 ml/1 tbsp lemon juice

Heat the oven to 190°C/375°F/gas 5.

Melt the margarine in a medium saucepan, add the onion and cook until softened, about 5 minutes. Add the oatmeal, stock and milk and bring to the boil, stirring all the time. Simmer for 20 minutes, until the oatmeal is tender. Remove from the heat and stir in the watercress, cheese, egg yolks, mustard, pepper and lemon juice.

Whisk the egg whites until stiff, then fold into the oatmeal mixture. Transfer to a greased 1.2 litre/2 pint soufflé dish or baking dish and bake for 30–35 minutes until well risen and golden brown. Serve immediately.

Country cheese pudding

Serves 4
**Per serving: 315 kcal, 1318 KJ, 19.2 protein, 19.3 g fat,
17.3 g carbohydrate, 0.7 g soluble fibre, 0.5 g insoluble fibre**

75 g/3 oz rolled oats
3 eggs, separated
300 ml/½ pint semi-skimmed milk
15 ml/1 tbsp dry mustard

5 ml/1 tsp paprika
5 ml/1 tsp Worcestershire sauce
150 g/5 oz red Leicester cheese, grated

Heat the oven to 200°C/400°F/gas 6.

Place the oats in a bowl with the egg yolks. Warm the milk and pour over the rolled oats, stirring well. Leave to soak for 10 minutes, then stir in the mustard, paprika, Worcestershire sauce and cheese.

Whisk the egg whites until stiff, then fold into the oat mixture. Turn the mixture into a greased 1.2 litre/2 pint ovenproof dish. Bake for 30–35 minutes, until well risen and golden brown. Serve immediately.

Vegetable bake with garlic and herb crumble

Serves 4
**Per serving: 322 kcal, 1343 KJ, 13 g protein, 22.8 g fat,
17 g carbohydrate, 1.8 g soluble fibre, 1.9 g insoluble fibre**

40 g/1½ oz polyunsaturated margarine
100 g/4 oz carrots, sliced
325 g/12 oz cauliflower, broken into
  florets
100 g/4 oz green beans, chopped into
  short lengths
25 g/1 oz plain flour
300 ml/½ pint semi-skimmed milk

salt and pepper
100 g/4 oz Gouda cheese, grated
25 g/1 oz rolled oats
25 g/1 oz chopped walnuts
15 ml/1 tbsp mixed chopped fresh
  herbs
15 ml/1 tbsp oil
1 clove garlic, crushed

Heat the oven to 190°C/375°F/gas 5.

Melt the margarine in a medium saucepan, add the vegetables and stir until well coated. Stir in the flour and cook for 1 minute. Gradually add the milk, stirring until the sauce is thickened and smooth.

Remove from the heat and stir in a little salt and pepper and 75 g/3 oz of the cheese. Transfer to an ovenproof dish.

Mix together the oats, nuts, herbs and remaining cheese. Heat the oil in a small pan and fry the garlic until softened, about 2 minutes. Remove from the heat and stir in the oat mixture. Sprinkle over the vegetable mixture. Bake for 35–40 minutes until the topping is crispy and the vegetables are tender.

Cashew nut and oat stir-fry

Serves 4
Per serving: 267 kcal, 1117 KJ, 7.8 g protein, 17.1 g fat,
21.9 g carbohydrate, 2.1 g soluble fibre, 2.3 g insoluble fibre

30 ml/2 tbsp sunflower oil
50 g/2 oz onion, chopped
100 g/4 oz red pepper, seeded and
 chopped
100 g/4 oz carrots, coarsely grated
100 g/4 oz green beans, chopped into
 short lengths

100 g/4 oz rolled oats
50 g/2 oz cashew nuts
300 ml/½ pint vegetable stock
5 ml/1 tsp soy sauce
pepper
50 g/2 oz grated Edam cheese

Heat the oil in a large frying pan, add the onion and fry over a high heat for 2 minutes, stirring all the time. Add the red pepper, carrots and beans and stir-fry for 3 minutes. Add the oats and nuts and stir for 1 minute. Add the stock, soy sauce and pepper and bring to the boil. Cover and simmer for 2–3 minutes, until the vegetables are tender, but with a crunch. Serve piping hot sprinkled with grated cheese.

Mushroom and artichoke pizza

Serves 4
Per serving: 381 kcal, 1604 KJ, 17.1 g protein, 15.5 g fat,
46.3 g carbohydrate, 3.1 g soluble fibre, 4.8 g insoluble fibre

1 quantity Oat Pizza Base, see page
 78
5 ml/1 tsp olive oil
425 g/15 oz can chopped tomatoes
10 ml/2 tsp dried oregano
50 g/2 oz onion, chopped
15 ml/1 tbsp tomato purée

salt and pepper
100 g/4 oz mushrooms
400 g/14 oz can artichoke hearts,
 drained
100 g/4 oz mozzarella cheese
15 ml/1 tbsp chopped parsley

Heat the oven to 200°C/400°F/gas 6.
 Roll out the risen dough to fit a greased 23 cm × 33 cm/9 × 13 inch shallow oblong tin. Brush with oil, cover and leave to rise for about 20 minutes, while you make the topping.
 Place the tomatoes in a saucepan with the oregano, onion, tomato purée, salt and pepper. Bring to the boil, then simmer, uncovered, for about 10 minutes until thickened. Cool slightly.
 Slice the mushrooms thinly. Slice each artichoke heart into four, slice the cheese. Spread the tomato sauce over the pizza base and arrange the mushrooms, artichoke hearts and cheese evenly over the top. Bake for 30–35 minutes, until the cheese has melted and the dough is crisp and golden. Garnish with chopped parsley.

Two-cheese pizza

Serves 4
Per serving: 461 kcal, 1934 KJ, 22.1 g protein, 23.5 g fat, 43.1 g carbohydrate, 1.7 g soluble fibre, 3.1 g insoluble fibre

1 quantity Oat Pizza Base, see page 78
5 ml/1 tsp oil
425 g/15 oz can chopped tomatoes
5 ml/1 tsp dried oregano
5 ml/1 tsp chopped basil leaves

15 ml/1 tbsp tomato purée
salt and pepper
175 g/6 oz mozzarella cheese
25 g/1 oz Parmesan cheese, grated

Heat the oven to 200°C/400°F/gas 6.

Roll out the risen dough to a 25 cm/10 inch round. Place on a greased baking sheet. Brush the dough with oil. Cover and leave to rise for 20 minutes, while you make the topping.

Place the tomatoes in a saucepan with the oregano, basil, tomato purée, salt and pepper. Bring to the boil, then simmer, uncovered for 10 minutes, until thickened. Cool slightly.

Slice the mozzarella thinly. Spread the tomato sauce over the pizza base. Arrange the cheese slices on top. Sprinkle with Parmesan cheese and bake for 30–35 minutes, until the cheese has melted and the dough is crisp and golden. Serve warm with a crunchy salad.

Mushroom and nut loaf

Serves 4
Per serving: 269 kcal, 1126 KJ, 9.4 g protein, 14.6 g fat, 26.8 g carbohydrate, 2.1 g soluble fibre, 2.5 g insoluble fibre

100 g/4 oz pecan nuts, finely chopped
175 g/6 oz mushrooms, finely chopped
100 g/4 oz rolled oats
100 g/4 oz carrots, grated
100 g/4 oz onion, chopped
30 ml/2 tbsp chopped parsley
5 ml/1 tsp chopped rosemary
pepper

5 ml/1 tsp concentrated vegetable stock
60 ml/4 tbsp boiling water
1 egg, beaten
150 ml/¼ pint set low-fat yoghurt
30 ml/2 tbsp chopped spring onions
1 clove garlic, crushed

Heat the oven to 190°C/375°F/gas 5.

Place the pecans, mushrooms, oats, carrots, onion and herbs in a large bowl. Mix well, then season with plenty of pepper. Dissolve the stock in the water and add to the dry mix with the egg. Stir well. Press the mixture lightly into a greased 1.2 litre/2 pint loaf tin and smooth the top. Cover with foil and bake for 35 minutes, until firm.

Mix together the yoghurt, spring onions and garlic. Slice the loaf thickly and serve hot or cold with the yoghurt sauce.

Savoury lentil pie

Serves 6
Per serving: 405 kcal, 1699 KJ, 12.5 g protein, 18.9 g fat,
49.2 g carbohydrate, 2.5 g soluble fibre, 3.6 g insoluble fibre

100 g/4 oz red lentils
50 g/2 oz carrots, chopped
75 g/3 oz onions, chopped
450 ml/¾ pint water
10 ml/2 tsp concentrated vegetable
  stock
100 g/4 oz coarse oatmeal

15 ml/1 tbsp tomato purée
5 ml/1 tsp mixed dried herbs
pepper
1½ quantities High Fibre Pastry,
  see page 120
15 ml/1 tbsp milk, for brushing
5 ml/1 tsp sesame seeds

Heat the oven to 200°C/400°F/gas 6.

Place the lentils, carrots, onions, water and stock in a pan. Bring
to the boil, then reduce heat, cover and simmer for 20–25
minutes, until the lentils are tender. Add the oatmeal, tomato
purée, herbs and pepper and simmer for a further 15 minutes.
Cool slightly.

Roll out just over half the pastry and line a 23 cm/9 inch pie
plate. Fill with the oatmeal mixture. Roll out the remaining pastry
and cover the pie, wetting the edges to seal. Trim off any excess
pastry and use to decorate the pie. Make a hole in the centre of the
pie, brush with milk and sprinkle with sesame seeds. Bake for 30–
35 minutes until the pastry is nicely browned.

Savoury oat loaf

Serves 4
Per serving: 279 kcal, 1164 KJ, 12.5 g protein, 18.5 g fat,
16.5 g carbohydrate, 1 g soluble fibre, 0.8 g insoluble fibre

2 onions, finely chopped
25 g/1 oz polyunsaturated margarine
75 g/3 oz rolled oats
125 g/5 oz mature Cheddar cheese,
  grated
30 ml/2 tbsp chopped parsley

5 ml/1 tsp mixed herbs
5 ml/1 tsp concentrated vegetable
  stock
pepper
1 egg, beaten

Heat the oven to 190°C/375°F/gas 5.

Fry the onions in the margarine until softened and slightly
browned, about 10 minutes. Remove from the heat and stir in the
oats, cheese, parsley, herbs, stock and pepper. Mix well.

Add the egg and mix thoroughly. Press lightly into a greased
450 g/1 lb loaf tin. Bake for 35 minutes until browned and crispy.
Turn out and serve hot or cold cut into thick slices. Serve with a
fresh tomato sauce and a crunchy salad.

Spinach and tomato soufflé

Serves 4

Per serving: 295 kcal, 1236 KJ, 16.3 g protein, 17 g fat, 20.6 g carbohydrate, 0.7 g soluble fibre, 0.5 g insoluble fibre

225 g/8 oz spinach
25 g/1 oz polyunsaturated margarine
100 g/4 oz onion, chopped
75 g/3 oz medium oatmeal
300 ml/½ pint semi-skimmed milk
5 ml/1 tsp yeast extract

175 g/6 oz tomatoes, chopped
75 g/3 oz Cheddar cheese, grated
pinch grated nutmeg
pepper
2 eggs, separated

Heat the oven to 190°C/375°F/gas 5.

Wash the spinach thoroughly. Place in a pan with no extra water and cook, covered, for about 5 minutes, until tender. Strain through a sieve, pressing out as much water as possible, then chop finely.

Melt the margarine in a saucepan, add the onion and fry for about 5 minutes, until softened. Stir in the oatmeal, then add the milk and yeast extract and bring to the boil. Simmer for 20 minutes, stirring occasionally. Remove from the heat and add the spinach, tomatoes, cheese, nutmeg, pepper and egg yolks. Mix well.

Whisk the egg whites until stiff, then fold into the oatmeal mixture. Transfer to a greased 1.2 litre/2 pint soufflé dish and bake for 30–35 minutes, until well risen and golden brown. Serve immediately.

Summer stir-fry (*above*, see page 55); Spinach and tomato soufflé (*below*).
OVERLEAF Crunchy salad (*top left*, see page 50);
Bacon and leek flan (*bottom left*, see page 87);
Leg of lamb stuffed with apricot and lemon with Crunchy roast potatoes (*right*, see pages 80 and 88).

Courgette and mushroom cheesecake

Serves 8
Per serving: 240 kcal, 999 KJ, 14.4 g protein, 16.5 g fat,
8.9 g carbohydrate, 0.4 g soluble fibre, 0.6 g insoluble fibre

50 g/2 oz wholewheat breadcrumbs
50 g/2 oz medium oatmeal
50 g/2 oz polyunsaturated margarine
225 g/8 oz low-fat soft cheese with
garlic and herbs
3 eggs, separated

175 g/6 oz mozzarella cheese, grated
or finely chopped
150 ml/¼ pint natural low-fat yoghurt
100 g/4 oz courgettes, grated
100 g/4 oz mushrooms, chopped
salt and pepper

Heat the oven to 160°C/325°F/gas 3.

Mix together the breadcrumbs and oatmeal. Melt the margarine and stir in well. Press into the base of a greased 20 cm/8 inch loose-based cake tin.

Beat together the low-fat cheese and egg yolks. Beat in the mozzarella cheese, yoghurt, courgettes, mushrooms and seasoning. Whisk the egg whites until stiff. Fold into the cheese mixture with a metal spoon. Turn into the cake tin and smooth the top.

Bake for 40–45 minutes until golden brown and firm to the touch. Cool in the tin for 10 minutes, then loosen the edges with a knife and remove from tin. Serve warm or cold.

Cheese and nut sausages

Serves 4
Per serving: 496 kcal, 2063 KJ, 21.4 g protein, 37.3 g fat,
20 g carbohydrate, 1.1 soluble fibre, 1 g insoluble fibre

50 g/2 oz chopped walnuts
225 g/8 oz Caerphilly cheese, grated
100 g/4 oz medium oatmeal
5 ml/1 tsp Dijon mustard

5 ml/1 tsp paprika
100 ml/3 fl oz milk
1 egg
30 ml/2 tbsp oil

Mix together the walnuts, cheese, 75 g/3 oz of the oatmeal, the mustard and paprika. Add the milk and mix until firm. Divide into eight equal pieces and shape each piece into a sausage.

Beat the egg on a plate with 15 ml/1 tbsp water. Coat the sausages in egg, then in the remaining oatmeal. Chill for 30 minutes.

Heat the oil in a large frying pan, add the sausages and fry on all sides until crisp and golden brown. Drain on kitchen paper and serve warm.

Cheese and nut sausages (*above*); Courgette and mushroom cheesecake (*below*).

Oatmeal and cheese wedges

Serves 4
Per serving: 281 kcal, 1170 KJ, 11.9 g protein, 19 g fat,
16.6 g carbohydrate, 1.3 g soluble fibre, 1 g insoluble fibre

225 g/8 oz onion, grated
30 ml/2 tbsp sunflower oil
75 g/3 oz fine oatmeal
10 ml/2 tsp concentrated vegetable
  stock

150 ml/¼ pint boiling water
75 g/3 oz Gruyère cheese, grated
30 ml/2 tbsp Parmesan cheese, grated
salt and pepper
1 egg, beaten

Heat the oven to 190°C/375°F/gas 5.

Fry the onion in the oil until softened, about 5 minutes. Add the oatmeal and stir well. Dissolve the stock in the boiling water and add to the pan. Return to the boil, then simmer for 15 minutes.

Remove from the heat and stir in the cheeses, salt, pepper and egg. Press lightly into a greased 20 cm/8 inch sandwich tin. Bake for 30 minutes until lightly browned. Serve hot cut into wedges with jacket potatoes and a green vegetable.

Oat and lentil patties

Serves 4
Per serving: 310 kcal, 1310 KJ, 17.9 protein, 7.4 g fat,
45.7 g carbohydrate, 1.7 g soluble fibre, 2.8 g insoluble fibre

225 g/8 oz red lentils
5 ml/1 tsp curry powder
600 ml/1 pint water
1 medium onion, finely chopped
15 ml/1 tbsp lemon juice
15 ml/1 tbsp chopped parsley

15 ml/1 tbsp tomato paste
salt and pepper
75 g/3 oz medium oatmeal
1 egg, beaten
30 ml/2 tbsp sunflower oil, for shallow
  frying

Rinse the lentils and place in a pan with the curry powder and water. Bring to the boil then simmer, partially covered, for about 20 minutes, until the lentils are tender. Add the onion, lemon juice, parsley, tomato paste, salt and pepper and mix well. Cook gently, stirring for 5 minutes. Remove from heat and stir in half the oatmeal. Leave to cool.

Shape the cold mixture into eight patties and coat in egg and the remaining oatmeal, pressing it on firmly. Heat a little oil in a large frying pan and fry the patties for 8–10 minutes, turning once, until golden brown. Serve piping hot with pitta bread, natural yoghurt and steamed vegetables or a crunchy salad.

Vegetable burgers

Serves 4
Per serving: 350 kcal, 1459 KJ, 10.2 g protein, 23.8 g fat,
25.4 g carbohydrate, 2.2 g soluble fibre, 1.6 g insoluble fibre

45 ml/3 tbsp sunflower oil
1 medium onion, grated
1 medium carrot, grated
1 celery stick, finely chopped
1 clove garlic, crushed
50 g/2 oz oat bran and oat germ
75 g/3 oz rolled oats

50 g/2 oz strong Cheddar cheese,
grated
30 ml/2 tbsp milk
1 egg, beaten
salt and pepper
oat bran and oat germ, to coat
sunflower oil, for shallow frying

Heat half the oil, add the vegetables and garlic and fry until softened, about 5 minutes. Remove from heat and cool. Mix the oat bran and oat germ with the rolled oats. Stir in the vegetables, cheese, milk, egg and seasoning. Mix well.

Shape into eight rounds and coat in oat bran and oat germ. Fry in the remaining oil for 10 minutes, turning once until crispy and browned. Serve with home-made tomato sauce.

Oat and courgette bake

Serves 4
Per serving: 329 kcal, 1370 KJ, 14.2 g protein, 24.6 g fat,
13.6 carbohydrate, 1.4 g soluble fibre, 1.4 g insoluble fibre

1 medium onion, chopped
15 ml/1 tbsp sunflower oil
350 g/12 oz courgettes, sliced
225 g/8 oz tomatoes, skinned and
chopped

salt and pepper
50 g/2 oz rolled oats
175 g/6 oz Gouda cheese, grated
25 g/1 oz polyunsaturated margarine

Heat the oven to 180°C/350°F/gas 4.

Fry the onion in the oil until softened and lightly browned, about 5 minutes.

Arrange half the courgettes and tomatoes in an oiled ovenproof dish. Season with salt and pepper and cover with half the onion. Mix together the oats, cheese and a little seasoning and sprinkle half this mixture over the vegetables. Repeat the layers. Dot the top with margarine, cover and bake for 45 minutes, removing the cover for the last 10 minutes to crisp the top. Serve piping hot with grilled mushrooms and watercress.

Broccoli oat crumble

Serves 4
Per serving: 415 kcal, 1726 KJ, 19.9 g protein, 27.8 g fat,
22.4 g carbohydrate, 3.2 g soluble fibre, 3.2 g insoluble fibre

675 g/1½ lb broccoli
50 g/2 oz butter or polyunsaturated
  margarine
25 g/1 oz plain flour
300 ml/½ pint milk
5 ml/1 tsp Dijon mustard
salt and pepper

125 g/5 oz mature Cheddar cheese,
  grated
50 g/2 oz rolled oats
15 ml/1 tbsp chopped parsley
25 g/1 oz raw peanuts, roughly
  chopped

Heat the oven to 200°C/400°F/gas 6.
   Cut off the broccoli florets. Peel the stems and slice them
thinly.
   Melt the butter in a pan, add the broccoli and turn until evenly
coated. Stir in the flour and cook for 1 minute. Gradually add the
milk, stirring until thickened and smooth. Add the mustard, salt
and pepper and mix well. Cover and cook gently for 10
minutes.
   Remove from the heat and stir in 100 g/4 oz of the cheese. Turn
into a buttered ovenproof dish. Mix together the remaining
cheese, oats, parsley and peanuts. Sprinkle evenly over the top.
Bake for 15–20 minutes until the topping is crisp and the cheese
has melted.

Farmhouse cheese pudding

Serves 4
Per serving: 341 kcal, 1421 KJ, 16.2 g protein, 22.5 g fat,
19.5 g carbohydrate, 1.2 g soluble fibre, 1 g soluble fibre

25 g/1 oz polyunsaturated margarine
1 medium onion, chopped
100 g/4 oz medium oatmeal
10 ml/2 tsp concentrated vegetable
  stock

300 ml/½ pint boiling water
150 g/5 oz mature Cheddar cheese,
  grated
salt and pepper
2 eggs, separated

Heat the oven to 190°C/375°F/gas 5.
   Melt the margarine in a saucepan. Add the onion and fry until
softened, about 5 minutes. Add the oatmeal and stir well.
   Dissolve the stock in the boiling water and add to the pan. Bring
back to the boil, then simmer for 30 minutes, stirring occasionally,
until thickened. Remove from the heat and stir in the cheese, salt,
pepper and egg yolks.

Whisk the egg whites until stiff and fold carefully into the oat mixture. Turn into a greased 1.2 litre/2 pint ovenproof dish. Bake for 30–35 minutes until well risen and golden brown. Serve straight from the oven with a selection of vegetables. Cauliflower, green beans, aubergine and sweetcorn go well.

Carrot and oatmeal pie

Serves 4
Per serving: 318 kcal, 1328 KJ, 10.1 g protein, 20 g fat, 26 g carbohydrate, 2.3 g soluble fibre, 1.8 g insoluble fibre

225 g/8 oz onion, grated
225 g/8 oz carrots, grated
50 g/2 oz butter or polyunsaturated margarine, melted
75 g/3 oz mature Cheddar cheese, grated
100 g/4 oz rolled oats
salt and pepper
5 ml/1 tsp oregano
150 ml/¼ pint milk

Heat the oven to 190°C/375°F/gas 5.

Mix together the onion and carrots. Stir in half the melted fat. In another bowl mix together the cheese, oats, salt, pepper and oregano. Layer the vegetable and oat mixtures in a greased 1.2 litre/2 pint pie dish, starting and finishing with the oat mixture. Pour over the milk, then drizzle over the remaining melted fat.

Bake for 30–40 minutes until the topping is crisp and golden brown. Serve hot with vegetables or a crispy salad.

Savoury potato bake

Serves 4
Per serving: 342 kcal, 1446 KJ, 20 g protein, 10.7 g fat, 44.4 g carbohydrate, 1.7 g soluble fibre, 1.3 g insoluble fibre

675 g/1½ lb potatoes, steamed in their skins
4 spring onions, chopped
45 ml/3 tbsp chopped parsley
salt and pepper
300 ml/½ pint low-fat soft cheese
50 g/2 oz medium oatmeal, toasted
50 g/2 oz Gruyère cheese, grated
5 ml/1 tsp paprika
2 eggs, separated

Heat the oven to 190°C/375°F/gas 5.

Slice the potatoes and arrange in an oiled ovenproof dish. Sprinkle with onions, parsley, salt and pepper. Beat together the soft cheese, oatmeal, cheese and paprika. Season with salt and pepper and stir in the egg yolks.

Whisk the egg whites until stiff, then fold into the cheese mixture. Spread over the potatoes and bake for 30–35 minutes until the top is golden brown.

Creamy onion flan

Serves 4
Per serving: 525 kcal, 2186 KJ, 16.4 g protein, 38.2 g fat, 30.9 g carbohydrate, 2 g soluble fibre, 3.2 g insoluble fibre

1 quantity High Fibre Pastry, see
  page 120
25 g/1 oz polyunsaturated margarine
225 g/8 oz onions, chopped
100 g/4 oz Gruyère cheese, grated

2 eggs, beaten
150 ml/¼ pint soured cream
salt and pepper
15 ml/1 tbsp chopped parsley

Heat the oven to 200°C/400°F/gas 6.

Roll out the pastry and line a 20 cm/8 inch flan tin. Prick the base and bake blind for 10 minutes. Reduce the oven temperature to 180°C/350°F/gas 4.

Melt the margarine in a frying pan, add the onions and fry gently for 10 minutes until softened and lightly browned. Remove and cool slightly.

Spread the onions over the base of the flan and sprinkle with cheese. Mix together the eggs, cream, salt and pepper and pour into the flan case. Sprinkle with parsley and bake for 30 minutes until golden brown and firm to the touch. Serve warm or cold.

Bean croquettes

Serves 4
Per serving: 308 kcal, 1300 KJ, 16.8 g protein, 8.2 g fat, 44.5 g carbohydrate, 5.6 g soluble fibre, 6 g insoluble fibre

225 g/8 oz haricot beans, soaked
  overnight
50 g/2 oz onion, chopped
1 clove garlic, crushed
15 ml/1 tbsp sunflower oil
15 ml/1 tbsp lemon juice
5 ml/1 tsp ground cumin

5 ml/1 tsp ground coriander
2.5 ml/½ tsp chilli powder
25 g/1 oz oat bran and oat germ
salt and pepper
1 egg, beaten
75 g/3 oz medium oatmeal

Heat the oven to 200°C/400°F/gas 6.

Cook the beans in a saucepan with water to cover until tender, about 1 hour. Drain well.

Fry the onion and garlic in the oil until softened, about 5 minutes. Add the lemon juice and spices and cook for 2 minutes. Place the beans in a blender or food processor with the spice mixture. Purée until fairly smooth. Add the oat bran and oat germ, salt and pepper and mix well. Shape the mixture into croquettes, then coat in egg and oatmeal, pressing it on firmly. Place in an oiled baking dish and bake for 25–30 minutes, until golden brown. Serve with thick strained yoghurt flavoured with garlic and hot pitta bread.

Cheese and spinach pie

Serves 6
Per serving: 387 kcal, 1615 KJ, 18 g protein, 23.7 g fat,
26.9 g carbohydrate, 1.9 g soluble fibre, 3.7 g insoluble fibre

450 g/1 lb spinach
15 ml/1 tbsp sunflower oil
100 g/4 oz mushrooms, sliced
5 ml/1 tsp oregano
225 g/8 oz curd cheese
3 eggs, beaten

45 ml/3 tbsp milk
salt and pepper
1½ quantities High Fibre Pastry,
see page 120
milk, to glaze
10 ml/2 tsp sesame seeds

Heat the oven to 200°C/400°F/gas 6.

Wash the spinach in several changes of water. Place in a pan
with no extra water and cook, covered, until softened, about 5
minutes. Drain the spinach, pressing out as much water as possible. Chop finely.

Heat the oil in a small pan, add the mushrooms and fry gently
until softened. Stir in the oregano.

Beat the curd cheese until softened, then gradually beat in the
eggs. Stir in the spinach, mushrooms, milk and a little salt and
pepper.

Roll out just over half the pastry and line a 23 cm/9 inch flan tin.
Spread the filling over the top and damp the edges of the pastry.
Roll out the remaining pastry and cover the pie. Trim the edges
and pinch to seal. Make a hole in the centre of the pie. Brush with
milk and sprinkle with sesame seeds.

Bake for 40–45 minutes until the pastry is a rich brown and the
filling feels firm. The pastry will rise up during the cooking but
settle back as it cools. Cool slightly in the tin, then remove and
serve warm or cold.

Stuffed aubergines

Serves 4
Per serving: 396 kcal, 1646 KJ, 9.1 g protein, 33.7 g fat, 15.4 g carbohydrate, 3.1 g soluble fibre, 3.2 g insoluble fibre

2 large aubergines, about 675 g/1½ lb
45 ml/3 tbsp olive oil
1 onion, chopped
1 clove garlic, crushed
1 green pepper, seeded and chopped
225 g/8 oz tomatoes, skinned and chopped
30 ml/2 tbsp snipped chives
5 ml/1 tsp mixed herbs
salt and pepper

Topping:
75 g/3 oz chopped walnuts
25 g/1 oz oat bran and oat germ
50 g/2 oz mature Cheddar cheese, grated
150 ml/¼ pint single cream

Heat the oven to 180°C/350°F/gas 4.

Halve the aubergines lengthwise and scoop out the flesh. Chop the flesh into small pieces.

Heat the oil in a frying pan, add the onion and garlic and fry for 5 minutes. Add the aubergine flesh and green pepper and fry for 5 minutes more. Stir in the tomatoes, herbs, salt and pepper and mix well.

Place the aubergine shells in a greased ovenproof dish. Fill with the aubergine mixture and press down lightly. Mix together the topping ingredients and spread over the stuffing. Bake for 45 minutes. Serve warm.

Salmon roll (*above*, see page 77); Cauliflower crisp (*below*, see page 75).

MAIN MEALS AND VEGETABLE ACCOMPANIMENTS

Cauliflower crisp

Serves 4   See photograph, page 73
Per serving: 67 kcal, 283 KJ, 2.9 g protein, 3.6 g fat,
6.3 g carbohydrate, 1.2 g soluble fibre, 1.3 g insoluble fibre

450 g/1 lb cauliflower
15 g/½ oz polyunsaturated margarine
1 clove garlic, crushed
25 g/1 oz rolled oats
pepper
15 ml/1 tbsp lemon juice

Cut the cauliflower into florets and steam for 10–12 minutes, until just tender. Meanwhile, melt the margarine, add the garlic and oats and fry until lightly toasted. Season with pepper and stir in the lemon juice. Transfer the cauliflower to a warmed serving bowl and sprinkle the oat mixture over the top.

Haddock flan

Serves 4
Per serving: 408 kcal, 1707 KJ, 23.4 g protein, 21.6 g fat,
31.8 g carbohydrate, 1.6 g soluble fibre, 2.8 g insoluble fibre

1 quantity High Fibre Pastry, see
  page 120
225 g/8 oz fresh haddock fillet
100 g/4 oz smoked haddock
30 ml/2 tbsp chopped spring onions
30 ml/2 tbsp chopped parsley
150 ml/¼ pint semi-skimmed milk
1 egg, beaten
pepper
25 g/1 oz Cheddar cheese, grated

Heat the oven to 190°C/375°F/gas 5.
  Roll out the pastry and line a 20 cm/8 inch flan case. Chill while preparing the filling.
  Place the fish on a heatproof plate and cover. Place over a pan of simmering water and steam for 10–12 minutes, until tender. Remove any skin and bones and flake the fish. Cool slightly, then place in the flan case. Sprinkle with onions and parsley. Beat together the milk, egg and pepper and pour over the fish. Sprinkle with cheese. Bake for 35–40 minutes, until the top is lightly browned and the pastry is crisp.

Brie-stuffed chicken (*above*, see page 82); Chicken and apricot pies (*below*, see page 81).

Tuna and tomato fish cakes

Serves 4
Per serving: 264 kcal, 1109 KJ, 15.6 g protein, 13 g fat,
22.6 g carbohydrate, 1 g soluble fibre, 1 g insoluble fibre

198 g/7 oz can tuna in brine, drained *salt and pepper*
225 g/8 oz cooked potato *15 ml/1 tbsp wholewheat flour*
30 ml/2 tbsp lemon juice *1 egg, beaten*
15 ml/1 tbsp chopped spring onion *50 g/2 oz Toasted Oats, see page 49*
15 ml/1 tbsp tomato purée

Flake the fish finely and place in a bowl. Mash the potato and add
to the fish with the lemon juice, onion, tomato purée, salt and
pepper. Shape the mixture into a roll with floured hands, then
slice off into eight cakes. Coat the cakes in egg, then toasted oats,
pressing them firmly on to the surface. Chill the cakes for 30
minutes.

Place the cakes under a moderate grill for 15 minutes, turning
once during the cooking time.

Oatmeal-stuffed trout

Serves 4
Per serving: 502 kcal, 2103 KJ, 60.9 g protein, 24.5 g fat,
10 g carbohydrate, 0.7 g soluble fibre, 0.9 g insoluble fibre

4 trout, about 325 g/12 oz each, *2.5 ml/½ tsp grated orange rind*
  gutted *25 g/1 oz almonds, chopped*
salt and pepper *25 g/1 oz butter or polyunsaturated*
50 g/2 oz medium oatmeal *margarine*
15 ml/1 tbsp chopped parsley *15 ml/1 tbsp oil*
5 ml/1 tsp chopped dill *50 g/2 oz onion, chopped*

Heat the oven to 190°C/375°F/gas 5.

Remove the heads from the trout. Open the fish out and place
on a board, skin side up. Press firmly all along the backbone, then
using a sharp pointed knife, lift out the bones. Season the flesh
with a little salt and pepper.

In a bowl, mix the oatmeal, parsley, dill, orange rind and
almonds. Melt the butter or margarine and half the oil and fry the
onion until softened, about 5 minutes. Stir into the dry
ingredients, mixing well.

Stuff the trout with the oatmeal mixture and secure with cocktail sticks. Place in an oiled baking dish and brush with the remaining oil. Cover with foil and bake for 25–30 minutes until the trout
are tender.

Salmon roll

Serves 6   See photograph, page 73
**Per serving: 340 kcal, 1422 KJ, 12.8 g protein, 20.5 g fat,
28 g carbohydrate, 1.6 g soluble fibre, 2.6 g insoluble fibre**

25 g/1 oz polyunsaturated margarine   *50 g/2 oz Toasted Oats, see page 49*
100 g/4 oz onions, chopped   *pepper*
175 g/6 oz mushrooms, sliced   *60 ml/4 tbsp soured cream*
175 g/6 oz tomatoes, chopped   *1 quantity High Fibre Pastry, see*
198 g/7 oz can salmon, drained and   *page 120*
* flaked*   *15 ml/1 tbsp milk, to glaze*

Heat the oven to 200°C/400°F/gas 6.

Melt the margarine in a saucepan, add the onions and fry until softened, about 5 minutes. Add the mushrooms, and fry for a further 2 minutes. Remove from the heat and add the tomatoes, salmon, oats and pepper. Mix well, then fold in the soured cream.

Roll out the pastry to an oblong 30 cm × 20 cm/12 × 8 inches. Pile the filling down the centre of the pastry to within 1 cm/½ inch of the ends. Brush the edges with milk and fold pastry over the filling to enclose it. Seal the edges. Decorate the roll with any pastry trimmings. Brush with the milk and bake for 30 minutes until the pastry is crisp and golden brown.

American hot pizza

Serves 4
Per serving: 296 kcal, 1246 KJ, 8.8 g protein, 10.9 g fat,
43.3 carbohydrate, 1.8 g soluble fibre, 3.2 g insoluble fibre

1 quantity Oat Pizza Base, see
  below
5 ml/1 tsp sunflower oil
425 g/15 oz can chopped tomatoes
1 clove garlic, crushed
25 g/1 oz green chillies, halved and
  seeded

15 ml/1 tbsp tomato purée
5 ml/1 tsp honey
salt and pepper
50 g/2 oz cabano or peperoni sausage,
  thinly sliced
1 red pepper, chopped
50 g/2 oz black olives

Heat the oven to 200°C/400°F/gas 6.

Roll out the risen dough to a 25 cm/10 inch round. Place on a greased baking sheet. Brush with oil, cover and leave to rise for 20 minutes, while you prepare the topping.

Place the tomatoes in a saucepan with the garlic, chillies, tomato purée, honey, salt and pepper. Bring to the boil, then simmer, uncovered, for about 10 minutes, until thickened. Cool slightly.

Spread the tomato sauce over the pizza base. Arrange the cabanos, pepper and olives on top. Bake for 30–35 minutes until the base is golden brown and crisp.

Oat pizza base

Makes 2
Per base: 463 kcal, 1961 KJ, 14.3 g protein, 11.4 g fat,
81 g carbohydrate, 2.6 g soluble fibre, 4.8 g insoluble fibre

10 ml/2 tsp dried yeast
5 ml/1 tsp sugar
150 ml/¼ pint warm water
175 g/6 oz 85% wholewheat flour

50 g/2 oz medium oatmeal
2.5 ml/½ tsp salt
15 ml/1 tbsp sunflower oil

Sprinkle the yeast and sugar into the water, stir to mix and leave in a warm place until frothy, about 10 minutes. Mix the flour, oatmeal and salt in a large bowl. Make a well in the centre and add the yeast liquid and oil. Mix to form a soft dough. Knead on a lightly floured surface for 5 minutes, until soft and pliable. Cover the dough with oiled polythene and leave to rise until doubled in size, about 45 minutes. Knead the dough briefly until firm. Use as required.

Pot roasted chicken with oat stuffing

Serves 4

Per serving: 592 kcal, 2483 KJ, 60 g protein, 28.2 g fat,
26.1 g carbohydrate, 1.8 g soluble fibre, 1.2 g insoluble fibre

5 ml/1 tsp grated lemon rind
100 g/4 oz medium oatmeal
50 g/2 oz polyunsaturated margarine,
  melted
100 g/4 oz onion, finely chopped
salt and pepper
45 ml/3 tbsp chopped parsley
1.8 kg/4 lb roasting chicken
15 ml/1 tbsp sunflower oil

75 g/3 oz carrot, chopped
75 g/3 oz celery, chopped
100 g/4 oz potato, chopped
2 cloves
30 ml/2 tbsp lemon juice
1 bay leaf
300 ml/½ pint chicken stock or
  water

Mix together the lemon rind, oatmeal, margarine, onion, salt,
pepper and parsley. Stuff the neck end of the chicken with the
mixture. Heat the oil in a flameproof casserole or heavy-based
saucepan which will fit the bird snugly. Add the chicken and fry all
over until evenly browned. Add the carrot, celery, potato, cloves,
lemon juice, bay leaf and stock and bring to the boil. Cover tightly
and simmer for 1–1¼ hours until the chicken is tender. Remove
the chicken from the pan and place on a warmed serving plate.

Skim off any surface fat from the pan juices, then sieve them
into a small pan, pressing through as much of the vegetable mixture as possible. Reheat the sauce, adding a little salt and
pepper if necessary.

Apple and celery stuffing

Serves 6

Per serving: 94 kcal, 398 KJ, 2.1 g protein, 3.6 g fat,
14.3 carbohydrate, 1.2 g soluble fibre, 1.1 g insoluble fibre

15 ml/1 tbsp sunflower oil
175 g/6 oz onion, chopped finely
75 g/3 oz celery, chopped finely
225 g/8 oz cooking apples, peeled,
  cored and chopped

75 g/3 oz rolled oats
30 ml/2 tbsp chopped parsley
salt and pepper

Heat the oil in a saucepan, add the onion and celery and fry gently
for about 5 minutes, until softened. Add the apples, cover the pan
and cook for 2 minutes, until slightly softened. Remove from the
heat then stir in the oats, parsley, salt and pepper. Use to stuff a
duck or chicken.

Apricot and lemon stuffing

Serves 6   See photograph, page 63
Per serving: 85 kcal, 360 KJ, 3.1 g protein, 2 g fat,
14.5 g carbohydrate, 1 g soluble fibre, 0.7 g insoluble fibre

75 g/3 oz dried no–soak apricots   *1 clove garlic, crushed*
75 g/3 oz rolled oats   *30 ml/2 tbsp lemon juice*
2.5 ml/½ tsp ground cumin   *salt and pepper*
2.5 ml/½ tsp ground coriander   *1 egg, beaten*

Chop the apricots finely and mix with the oats, cumin, coriander
and garlic. Moisten with lemon juice and season lightly with salt
and pepper. Stir in the egg and use to stuff a boned leg of lamb, or
chicken. Double this quantity to stuff a turkey.

Nut and mushroom stuffing

Serves 6
Per serving: 172 kcal, 716 KJ, 3.6 g protein, 13.2 g fat,
10.2 g carbohydrate, 0.8 g soluble fibre, 0.8 g insoluble fibre

100 g/4 oz walnuts, chopped   *25 g/1 oz polyunsaturated margarine,*
50 g/2 oz mushrooms, chopped   *melted*
2.5 ml/½ tsp mixed dried herbs   *30 ml/2 tbsp milk*
15 ml/1 tbsp chopped parsley   *salt and pepper*
75 g/3 oz medium oatmeal

Place all the ingredients in a bowl and stir well until evenly mixed.
Use to stuff a chicken or rolled inside flat fish fillets, or make into
small balls and bake in the oven to serve with chops or
vegetarian meals.

Oatmeal and onion stuffing

Serves 6
Per serving: 139 kcal, 583 KJ, 2.2 g protein, 8.6 g fat,
14 g carbohydrate, 0.8 g soluble fibre, 0.6 g insoluble fibre

100 g/4 oz medium oatmeal   *1 medium onion, finely chopped*
50 g/2 oz shredded vegetable suet *salt and pepper*

Toast the oatmeal lightly under a moderate grill or in the oven.
Mix with the suet, onion, salt and pepper. Stuff the neck end of
the chicken and roast or pot roast.

Chicken and apricot pies

Makes 12 See photograph, page 74
Per pie: 235 kcal, 983 KJ, 8.8 g protein, 13 g fat, 22.2 g carbohydrate, 1.4 g soluble fibre, 2.1 g insoluble fibre

225 g/8 oz boned chicken breast
15 g/½ oz polyunsaturated margarine
75 g/3 oz onion, finely chopped
75 g/3 oz dried no–soak apricots,
  finely chopped
30 ml/2 tbsp chopped parsley
5 ml/1 tsp chopped thyme

60 ml/4 tbsp set low-fat yoghurt
pepper
double quantity High Fibre Pastry,
  see page 120
15 ml/1 tbsp milk, to glaze
15 ml/1 tbsp medium oatmeal

Heat the oven to 200°C/400°F/gas 6.
Chop the chicken into small pieces. Heat the margarine in a medium pan, add the onion and fry gently until softened, about 5 minutes. Add the chicken and cook until sealed all over, about 5 minutes. Remove from the heat and stir in the apricots, herbs and yoghurt. Season with pepper.
Roll out two-thirds of the pastry and cut into rounds to line twelve deep bun tins. Fill with the chicken mixture. Brush the edges of the pastry with milk. Roll out the remaining pastry and cut into rounds to make lids, pressing the edges together to seal.
Make a hole in the centre of each pie. Brush with milk and sprinkle with oatmeal. Bake for 30 minutes until the pastry is golden and crisp. Serve warm or cold.

Spicy beef patties

Serves 4
Per serving: 330 kcal, 1373 KJ, 23.1 g protein, 21.8 g fat, 10.7 g carbohydrate, 0.5 g soluble fibre, 0.4 g insoluble fibre

450 g/1 lb lean minced beef
100 g/4 oz onion, finely chopped
5 ml/1 tsp grated lemon rind

50 g/2 oz fine oatmeal
15 ml/1 tbsp soy sauce
10 ml/2 tsp sunflower oil

Place the beef, onion, lemon rind, oatmeal and soy sauce in a bowl. Mix thoroughly until all the ingredients are well mixed. Divide into four or eight pieces and shape into flat rounds. Brush with oil and place under a moderate grill for 10–12 minutes, turning once. Serve with a salad and jacket potatoes.

Crunchy chicken drumsticks

Serves 4
Per serving: 256 kcal, 1074 KJ, 26.3 g protein, 12.5 g fat,
10.1 carbohydrate, 0.5 g soluble fibre, 0.4 g insoluble fibre

50 g/2 oz medium oatmeal
5 ml/1 tsp finely grated orange rind
salt and pepper
30 ml/2 tbsp finely chopped parsley
1 egg, beaten

30 ml/2 tbsp cold water
8 chicken drumsticks, about 75 g/3 oz
    each
a little flour
sunflower oil, for deep frying

Mix together the oatmeal, orange rind, salt, pepper and parsley.
Mix the egg with the water on a plate.
   Dry the chicken thoroughly with kitchen paper, then toss
lightly in flour. Dip in the egg, then coat in the oatmeal mixture.
Chill the drumsticks before frying if time allows.
   Heat the oil to 180°C/350°F, then fry the chicken for 10–12
minutes until the coating is crisp and the chicken tender. Drain on
kitchen paper.

Brie–stuffed chicken

Serves 4   See photograph, page 74
Per serving: 354 kcal, 1470 KJ, 18.5 g protein, 27.2 g fat,
9.1 g carbohydrate, 0.5 g soluble fibre, 0.4 g insoluble fibre

4 boned chicken breasts, with skin,
    about 100 g/4 oz each
175 g/6 oz Brie
salt and pepper
a little flour
1 egg, beaten

30 ml/2 tbsp cold water
50 g/2 oz medium oatmeal
50 g/2 oz butter or polyunsaturated
    margarine
15 ml/1 tbsp sunflower oil

Heat the oven to 220°C/425°F/gas 7.
   Loosen the skin from the chicken breasts, then place a slice of
Brie between the skin and flesh. Smooth the skin down to give a
good shape. Dry the chicken with kitchen paper, then toss lightly
in seasoned flour.
   Mix the egg with the water on a plate. Place the oatmeal on
another plate and season well with salt and pepper. Coat the
chicken in egg, then oatmeal. Chill at this stage for 30 minutes.
   Heat the butter and oil in a large roasting tin. Add the chicken
and baste well. Bake for 10 minutes, then reduce the temperature
to 180°C/350°F/gas 4 and cook for a further 20–25 minutes, until
the chicken is tender and the coating is crisp and golden. Serve hot
with cranberry sauce, mange tout and carrot sticks.

Oatmeal scotch eggs

Makes 4
Per egg: 320 kcal, 1332 KJ, 13 g protein, 25.3 g fat,
10.9 g carbohydrate, 0.2 g soluble fibre, 0.2 g insoluble fibre

4 eggs, hard boiled　　　　　　*1 egg, beaten*
a little flour　　　　　　　　*25 g/1 oz medium oatmeal*
225 g/8 oz sausagemeat　　　*sunflower oil, for deep frying*

Shell the eggs and toss in a little flour. Divide the sausagemeat into four and shape each piece evenly around an egg. Try to ensure that the sausagemeat is smooth with no visible cracks. Brush the 'eggs' with beaten egg and coat with oatmeal, pressing it well on. Chill for 30 minutes to set the coating.

Heat the fat or oil to 180°C/350°F. Fry the eggs for 6–8 minutes, until the coating is well browned. Drain well on kitchen paper and serve hot or cold.

Oat potato gratin

Serves 4
Per serving: 376 kcal, 1585 KJ, 9.4 g protein, 15.9 g fat,
52.2 g carbohydrate, 1.8 g soluble fibre, 1.3 g insoluble fibre

900 g/2 lb floury potatoes　　*75 ml/3 fl oz milk*
salt and pepper　　　　　　　*50 g/2 oz grated Gruyère*
freshly grated nutmeg　　　　*25 g/1 oz medium oatmeal*
50 g/2 oz butter

Peel the potatoes and cut them into evenly sized pieces. Cook in salted water until tender, then drain well and return to the pan to dry them out. Mash the potatoes until smooth, then season with pepper and nutmeg.

Melt the butter in the milk and beat into the potato until smooth and creamy. Transfer to a warmed gratin dish or shallow ovenproof dish and fork up the top. Sprinkle with cheese and oatmeal and place under a moderate grill until the top is golden brown.

Potato oatcakes

Serves 4
Per serving: 265 kcal, 1129 KJ, 7 g protein, 3.9 g fat,
54 g carbohydrate, 2.4 g soluble fibre, 1.8 g insoluble fibre

450 g/1 lb cooked, sieved potatoes
175 g/6 oz fine oatmeal
salt

Mix together the potatoes, oatmeal and salt to form a firm dough.
Roll out thinly on a floured surface. Cut into 8 cm/3 inch rounds
and prick with a fork.
   Heat a griddle or lightly oiled heavy frying pan. Cook the potato
oatcakes for 3–4 minutes on each side, until golden brown. Serve
warm as an accompaniment to a main meal or, wrapped in a clean
napkin, with a cooked breakfast. Spread lightly with butter or
margarine if you like.

Traditional meat loaf

Serves 6
Per serving: 390 kcal, 1622 KJ, 22.5 g protein, 29 g fat,
10.3 g carbohydrate, 0.8 soluble fibre, 0.6 insoluble fibre

225 g/8 oz streaky bacon, derinded   *30 ml/2 tbsp chopped parsley*
450 g/1 lb lean minced beef   *5 ml/1 tsp mixed herbs*
1 medium onion, chopped finely   *15 ml/1 tbsp Worcestershire sauce*
50 g/2 oz open mushrooms, chopped   *15 ml/1 tbsp tomato purée*
75 g/3 oz coarse oatmeal   *salt and pepper*
1 egg, beaten

Heat the oven to 180°C/350°F/gas 4.
   Stretch half the rashers with the back of a knife. Use to line the
base and sides of a 1.2 litre/2 pint loaf tin. Chop the remaining
bacon finely and mix with all the rest of the ingredients. Press the
mixture into the tin and smooth the top. Place in a roasting tin
half filled with hot water and bake for 50–60 minutes. Serve with
fresh tomato or mushroom sauce.

Oat bacon pudding

Serves 6
Per serving: 648 kcal, 2695 KJ, 15.1 g protein, 48.3 g fat,
40.6 g carbohydrate, 1.3 g soluble fibre, 3.6 g insoluble fibre

275 g/10 oz self-raising wholewheat flour
50 g/2 oz rolled oats
10 ml/2 tsp chopped thyme

175 g/6 oz vegetable suet
1 onion, peeled and chopped finely
325 g/12 oz streaky bacon, derinded and chopped

Place all the ingredients in a large bowl and stir well to mix. Add sufficient water to make a soft dough, then press lightly into a greased 1.2 litre/2 pint pudding basin. Cover with double thickness greased greaseproof paper and tie down. Steam for 2½ hours, then turn out and serve with a fresh tomato sauce.

Canadian beef pie

Serves 6
Per serving: 620 kcal, 2585 KJ, 24.3 g protein, 42 g fat,
39.2 g carbohydrate, 1.7 g soluble fibre, 4.9 g insoluble fibre

100 g/4 oz streaky bacon, derinded and finely chopped
50 g/2 oz onion, chopped
325 g/12 oz lean minced beef
50 g/2 oz mushrooms, chopped
1 egg, beaten
50 g/2 oz Cheddar cheese, grated
15 ml/1 tbsp chopped parsley

2.5 ml/½ tsp mixed dried herbs
25 g/1 oz medium oatmeal
salt and pepper
double quantity High Fibre Pastry, see page 120
milk, to glaze
oatmeal, to sprinkle

Heat the oven to 190°C/375°F/gas 5.

Place the bacon in a saucepan, heat gently until the fat starts to run. Add the onion and beef and fry gently, stirring all the time, until the beef is browned and separate. Drain off the excess fat and stir in the mushrooms. Remove from the heat and add the egg, cheese, parsley, herbs and oatmeal. Season with salt and pepper. Cool.

Roll out just over half the pastry and line a 23 cm/9 inch pie plate or flan tin. Fill with the meat mixture, pressing down lightly. Roll out the remaining pastry, brush the edges with water and cover the pie. Trim off the excess pastry and pinch the edges to seal. Make a small hole in the centre of the pie. Brush the top with milk and sprinkle with a little oatmeal. Bake for about 45 minutes, until the pastry is well browned. Serve hot or cold.

Lamb koftas

Serves 4
Per serving: 329 kcal, 1375 KJ, 19.6 g protein, 21.5 g fat,
15.2 g carbohydrate, 1.5 g soluble fibre, 1.5 g insoluble fibre

325 g/12 oz lean minced lamb   *5 ml/1 tsp ground allspice*
100 g/4 oz onion, grated   *salt and pepper*
50 g/2 oz medium oatmeal   *1 egg, beaten*
25 g/1 oz almonds, chopped   *25 g/1 oz medium oatmeal, for coating*
5 ml/1 tsp ground cinnamon

Heat the oven to 190°C/375°F/gas 5.
    Place the lamb, onion, oatmeal, almonds, spices, salt and pepper
in a bowl and mix well. Stir in the egg and mix until the mixture
binds together well. With damp hands, shape the mixture into
small balls (about sixteen), then roll in oatmeal to coat them.
Place the koftas a little apart in a roasting tin and bake for 20–25
minutes until lightly browned. Serve with a tomato sauce and
rice.

Sausage oat plait

Serves 6
Per serving: 456 kcal, 1901 KJ, 12.8 g protein, 31.8 g fat,
31.6 g carbohydrate, 1.2 g soluble fibre, 1.8 g insoluble fibre

100 g/4 oz self-raising wholewheat   Filling:
*   flour*   *450 g/1 lb sausagemeat*
50 g/2 oz medium oatmeal   *75 g/3 oz onion, grated*
5 ml/1 tsp baking powder   *5 ml/1 tsp chopped sage*
40 g/1½ oz polyunsaturated margarine   *50 g/2 oz medium oatmeal*
90 ml/6 tbsp milk   *salt and pepper*
milk, to glaze

Heat the oven to 200°C/400°F/gas 6.
    Place the flour, oatmeal and baking powder in a bowl. Add the
margarine, in small pieces, and rub in. Add the milk and mix to a
soft dough. Turn out on to a floured surface and knead lightly.
    Mix together all the filling ingredients. Roll out the dough to an
oblong 25 × 20 cm/10 × 8 inches. Pile the filling down the centre
of the dough to within 1 cm/½ inch of each end. Make diagonal
cuts either side of the filling at 2.5 cm/1 inch intervals.
    Brush the edges of the dough with milk, then lift strips of dough
over the filling alternately from each side to form a plait. Brush
the dough with milk and bake for 35–40 minutes, until evenly
browned. Serve warm or cold.

Bacon and leek flan

Serves 6   See photograph, page 62
Per serving: 366 kcal, 1520 KJ, 9.8 g protein, 27.3 g fat,
21.4 g carbohydrate, 1.5 g soluble fibre, 2.4 g insoluble fibre

1 quantity High Fibre Pastry, see   *225 g/8 oz leeks, sliced thinly*
*   page 120*   *150 ml/¼ pint soured cream*
15 ml/1 tbsp oil   *2 eggs, beaten*
100 g/4 oz streaky bacon, derinded   *salt and pepper*
*   and chopped*   *100 g/4 oz tomatoes, skinned*

Heat the oven to 200°C/400°F/gas 6.
   Roll out the pastry and line a 20 cm/8 inch flan tin. Bake blind
for 10 minutes then remove from the oven and reduce the temperature to 180°C/350°F/gas 4.
   Heat the oil in a frying pan, add the bacon and fry until lightly
browned, about 10 minutes. Add the leeks and fry until softened.
Spread over the flan case. Beat together the soured cream, eggs,
salt and pepper and pour into the flan case. Slice the tomatoes and
arrange on top. Bake for 30–35 minutes until the filling is set and
golden brown.

Curried lamb and potato patties

Serves 6
Per serving: 335 kcal, 1412 KJ, 15.8 g protein, 12.3 g fat,
42.3 g carbohydrate, 1.7 g soluble fibre, 2 g insoluble fibre

900 g/2 lb floury potatoes   *30 ml/2 tbsp tomato purée*
15 ml/1 tbsp sunflower oil   *15 ml/1 tbsp chopped mint*
175 g/6 oz onion, finely chopped   *salt and pepper*
5 ml/1 tsp grated root ginger   *1 egg, beaten*
225 g/8 oz lean minced lamb   *75 g/3 oz medium oatmeal*
5 ml/1 tsp garam masala   *30 ml/2 tbsp sunflower oil, for shallow*
5 ml/1 tsp ground coriander   *   frying*

Cook the potatoes until tender, drain them well, then return them
to the pan over a low heat until very dry. Mash well. Heat the oil in
a saucepan, add the onion and ginger and fry for 3 minutes, until
just softened. Add the lamb and stir over a moderate heat until
evenly browned, about 10 minutes. Add the garam masala and
coriander and cook for 1 minute. Stir in the tomato purée and
cook for 5 minutes more.
   Add the meat mixture to the potatoes with the mint, a pinch of
salt and a little pepper. Mix well. Form the mixture into small patties and coat in egg and oatmeal. Shallow fry for 6–8 minutes,
turning once, until golden brown. Serve with low-fat yoghurt
mixed with chopped cucumber and mint.

Crunchy roast potatoes

Serves 4   See photograph, page 63
Per serving: 288 kcal, 1220 KJ, 5.5 g protein, 8.3 g fat,
51.3 g carbohydrate, 1.8 g soluble fibre, 1.3 g insoluble fibre

900 g/2 lb evenly sized potatoes   *salt*
30 ml/2 tbsp sunflower oil   *25 g/1 oz coarse oatmeal*

Heat the oven to 190°C/375°F/gas 5.

Peel the potatoes and dry them. Make deep cuts down each
potato at 5 mm/¼ inch intervals almost to the base. Place the oil in
a roasting tin and heat in the oven for 5 minutes. Add the potatoes
and turn in the oil to coat them thinly. Arrange them cut sides
uppermost and sprinkle with a little salt and oatmeal. Bake for
1¼–1½ hours until the potatoes are golden brown.

DESSERTS

Carob and raspberry flan

Serves 4
Per serving: 367 kcal, 1530 KJ, 14 g protein, 23.2 g fat,
27 g carbohydrate, 1 g soluble fibre, 1.8 g insoluble fibre

75 g/3 oz Toasted Oats, see page 49
25 g/1 oz carob powder
25 g/1 oz soft light brown sugar
50 g/2 oz polyunsaturated margarine,
  melted
225 g/8 oz fresh or frozen raspberries
175 g/6 oz unflavoured fromage blanc
15 ml/1 tbsp clear honey

Mix together the oats, carob powder and sugar. Stir in the
margarine and mix well. Press into the base and sides of an 18 cm/
7 inch loose-based flan tin. Chill until firm.

Carefully remove the flan case from the tin and place on a serving plate. Lightly crush the raspberries and mix with the fromage
blanc and honey. Pile into the flan case and serve within 1
hour.

Carob and orange cheesecake

Serves 6
Per serving: 341 kcal, 1427 KJ, 12.3 g protein, 19.3 g fat,
31.4 g carbohydrate, 0.5 g soluble fibre, 0.4 g insoluble fibre

100 g/4 oz Toasted Oats, see page 49
50 g/2 oz polyunsaturated margarine,
  melted
30 ml/2 tbsp clear honey
225 g/8 oz curd cheese
2 eggs, separated
50 g/2 oz soft light brown sugar
15 g/1½ oz gelatine
45 ml/3 tbsp orange juice
50 g/2 oz bar carob
150 ml/¼ pint soured cream
15 ml/1 tbsp grated carob, to sprinkle

Mix together 75 g/3 oz oats, margarine and honey. Press into the
base of a greased 20 cm/8 inch loose-based cake tin.

Beat together the cheese, egg yolks and sugar. Sprinkle the
gelatine over the orange juice in a small bowl. Place in a pan of
simmering water until the gelatine has dissolved. Cool slightly,
then stir into the cheese mixture. Place the carob in a bowl then
place in the simmering water until it has melted. Stir into the
cheese mixture. Whisk the egg whites until stiff, then fold into the
cheese and carob mixture. Spread over the oat base. Chill until
firm.

Remove from the tin and spread the soured cream over the top.
Mix together remaining oats and grated carob. Sprinkle over the
soured cream.

Oatmeal ice cream

Serves 8
Per serving: 300 kcal, 1248 KJ, 3.7 g protein, 24.2 g fat,
17.9 g carbohydrate, 0.4 g soluble fibre, 0.3 g insoluble fibre

75 g/3 oz soft dark brown sugar   *150 ml/¼ pint single cream*
75 g/3 oz medium oatmeal   *2 eggs, separated*
300 ml/½ pint double cream   *5 ml/1 tsp vanilla essence*

Heat the oven to 200°C/400°F/gas 6. Set the freezer to the
coldest setting.

Mix together the sugar and oatmeal. Spread over a baking sheet
and bake for 10–15 minutes until toasted. Cool, then fork up the
mixture to separate it.

Whisk the double cream until stiff, then gradually whisk in the
single cream. Fold in the oatmeal mixture, egg yolks and
vanilla.

Whisk the egg whites until stiff. Fold into the cream mixture.
Pour into a polythene container and freeze until firm, about 3
hours. Transfer to the refrigerator 30 minutes before serving to
make it easier to scoop. Serve with fresh fruit.

Blackberry cobbler

Serves 4
Per serving: 361 kcal, 1524 KJ, 7.8 g protein, 12.4 g fat,
58.1 g carbohydrate, 2.5 g soluble fibre, 5.6 g insoluble fibre

675 g/1½ lb blackberries   *50 g/2 oz rolled oats*
50 g/2 oz soft brown sugar   *5 ml/1 tsp baking powder*
60 ml/4 tbsp apple juice   *5 ml/1 tsp ground cinnamon*
                                           50 g/2 oz polyunsaturated margarine
Cobbler: *25 g/1 oz soft brown sugar*
100 g/4 oz self-raising wholewheat   *75 ml/5 tbsp milk*
  flour

Heat the oven to 180°C/350°F/gas 4.

Mix together the blackberries, sugar and apple juice and place
in an ovenproof dish.

Mix the flour, oats, baking powder and cinnamon. Add the
margarine, in small pieces, and rub into the dry ingredients. Stir in
the sugar and milk and mix to a soft dough. Roll out to a 1 cm/½
inch thickness and cut into 5 cm/2 inch rounds. Arrange the
rounds, slightly overlapping over the fruit. Bake for 30–35
minutes until the cobbler is golden brown. Serve warm.

Blackberry cobbler (*above*); Oatmeal ice cream (*below*).

Baked apples

Serves 4
Per serving: 162 kcal, 687 KJ, 1.9 g protein, 2.8 g fat,
34.4 g carbohydrate, 1.5 g soluble fibre, 2.2 g insoluble fibre

4 cooking apples, about 175 g/6 oz   *30 ml/2 tbsp honey*
  each, cored   *25 g/1 oz chopped hazelnuts*
25 g/1 oz rolled oats   *2.5 ml/½ tsp mixed spice*
25 g/1 oz demerara sugar   *25 g/1 oz currants*

Heat the oven to 180°C/350°F/gas 4.
    Cut through the apple skins around the circumference and place the apples in a baking dish. Mix together the oats, sugar, honey, nuts, spice and currants. Stuff the apples with this mixture, piling it up if necessary. Put 60 ml/4 tbsp water in the dish. Cover with greaseproof paper and bake for 40–50 minutes, until the apples are tender.

Apricot, walnut and honey tart

Serves 8
Per serving: 242 kcal, 1014 KJ, 6.7 g protein, 13.1 g fat,
26 g carbohydrate, 1.3 g soluble fibre, 1.9 g insoluble fibre

1 quantity High Fibre Pastry, see   *150 ml/¼ pint natural low-fat*
  page 120   *yoghurt*
100 g/4 oz dried apricots, chopped   *60 ml/4 tbsp clear honey*
50 g/2 oz walnuts, chopped   *2.5 ml/½ tsp mixed spice*
2 eggs, beaten

Heat the oven to 200°C/400°F/gas 6.
    Roll out the pastry to line a 20 cm/8 inch flan tin or pie plate. Pinch the edges to decorate.
    Sprinkle the base of the pastry case with apricots and walnuts. Beat together the eggs, yoghurt, honey and spice. Pour into the pastry case and bake for 15 minutes, then reduce the heat to 180°C/350°F/gas 4 and cook for a further 30–35 minutes, until the pastry is crisp and the filling is set and golden brown. Serve warm or cold.

Apricot, walnut and honey tart (*top*); Apple layer pudding (*centre*, see page 98); Orange butterscotch pudding (*below*, see page 95).

Apricot pudding

Serves 6
Per serving: 353 kcal, 1474 KJ, 6.3 g protein, 21 g fat,
37.2 g carbohydrate, 1.6 g soluble fibre, 2.1 g insoluble fibre

100 g/4 oz polyunsaturated margarine　*few drops almond essence*
100 g/4 oz soft light brown sugar　*30 ml/2 tbsp milk*
2 eggs, beaten　*450 g/1 lb apricots, halved and stoned*
50 g/2 oz rolled oats　*15 ml/1 tbsp demerara sugar, to*
50 g/2 oz wholewheat flour　　*sprinkle*
50 g/2 oz ground almonds

Heat the oven to 180°C/350°F/gas 4.

Place the margarine, sugar, eggs, oats and flour in a bowl. Beat well until light and fluffy. Stir in the almonds, almond essence and milk.

Spread half the mixture over the base of a greased and lined 20 cm/8 inch loose-based cake tin. Arrange the apricots over the top and spread with the remaining cake mixture. Sprinkle with demerara sugar and bake for 40–50 minutes, until risen and golden brown. Turn out of the tin carefully and serve warm or cold.

American raisin pie

Serves 6
Per serving: 356 kcal, 1490 KJ, 7.2 g protein, 20.4 g fat,
38.3 g carbohydrate, 1.2 g soluble fibre, 2.1 g insoluble fibre

1 quantity High Fibre Pastry, see　*5 ml/1 tsp mixed spice*
　page 120　*2 eggs, beaten*
100 g/4 oz seedless raisins　*50 g/2 oz soft light brown sugar*
150 ml/¼ pint soured cream　*25 g/1 oz walnuts, chopped*

Heat the oven to 200°C/400°F/gas 6.

Roll out the pastry to line a deep, 20 cm/8 inch flan tin or pie plate. Prick the base and bake blind for 10 minutes. Reduce the oven temperature to 180°C/350°F/gas 4.

Mix together the raisins, soured cream, mixed spice, eggs, sugar and walnuts. Spread over the flan case and bake for 30–35 minutes, until the filling has set. Serve warm.

Coconut oat tart

Serves 6
**Per serving: 322 kcal, 1352 KJ, 5.2 g protein, 14.6 g fat,
45.3 carbohydrate, 1.3 g soluble fibre, 2.3 g insoluble fibre**

*1 quantity High Fibre Pastry, see
  page 120
50 g/2 oz Toasted Oats, see page 49
150 ml/¼ pint clear honey*

*2.5 ml/½ tsp grated lemon rind
30 ml/2 tbsp lemon juice
25 g/1 oz desiccated coconut*

Heat the oven to 200°C/400°F/gas 6.
  Roll out the pastry and line a 20 cm/8 inch pie plate or flan case.
Mix together the oats, honey, lemon rind, lemon juice and
coconut. Turn into the flan case and bake for 30–35 minutes, until
the pastry is crisp and golden. Serve with thick strained
yoghurt.

Orange butterscotch pudding

Serves 6   See photograph, page 92
**Per serving: 411 kcal, 1718 KJ, 6.6 g protein, 23.7 g fat,
45.6 g carbohydrate, 0.8 g soluble fibre, 1.8 g insoluble fibre**

Base:
*2 oranges
45 ml/3 tbsp fresh orange juice
50 g/2 oz butter or polyunsaturated
  margarine
25 g/1 oz soft light brown sugar*
Pudding:
100 g/4 oz polyunsaturated margarine

*100 g/4 oz soft light brown sugar
2 eggs
100 g/4 oz self-raising wholewheat
  flour
50 g/2 oz rolled oats
5 ml/1 tsp baking powder
60 ml/4 tbsp milk*

Heat the oven to 180°C/350°F/gas 4.
  Remove all the peel and white pith from the oranges. Cut the
oranges into thin slices. Grease a 20 cm/8 inch cake tin (not loose-
based) and line it with non-stick paper. Heat together the orange
juice, butter or margarine and sugar until the butter or margarine
has melted. Pour into the tin. Arrange the orange slices over
the top.
  Place all the pudding ingredients in a bowl and beat well with a
wooden spoon or mixer for 2–3 minutes. Place spoonfuls of mixture into the tin and smooth the top. Bake for 45–50 minutes until
risen and firm to the touch. Cool in the tin for 2 minutes, then turn
out on to a warm plate and serve warm with yoghurt.

Cranberry and raisin tart

Serves 6
Per serving: 292 kcal, 1229 KJ, 4.9 g protein, 11.6 g fat,
44.9 g carbohydrate, 2.5 g soluble fibre, 4.2 g insoluble fibre

1 quantity High Fibre Pastry, see   *75 g/3 oz seedless raisins*
*   page 120*   *60 ml/4 tbsp orange juice*
225 g/8 oz fresh or frozen cranberries   *30 ml/2 tbsp fine oatmeal*
75 g/3 oz soft light brown sugar

Heat the oven to 200°C/400°F/gas 6.
    Roll out the pastry thinly to line a 20 cm/8 inch flan tin and
reserve the trimmings.
    Mix together the cranberries, sugar, raisins, orange juice and
oatmeal. Spread over the pastry case. Roll out the trimmings and
cut into thin strips. Place a lattice of pastry over the tart, dampen-
ing the ends to make them stick. Bake for 35–40 minutes, until
the pastry is golden brown. Serve warm or cold.

Crunchy cheesecake

Serves 6
Per serving: 346 kcal, 1450 KJ, 9.5 g protein, 17.2 g fat,
40.6 g carbohydrate, 0.9 g soluble fibre, 1.3 g insoluble fibre

75 g/3 oz rolled oats   Filling:
75 g/3 oz wholewheat flour   *225 g/8 oz low-fat soft cheese*
50 g/2 oz demerara sugar   *50 g/2 oz light muscovado sugar*
100 g/4 oz polyunsaturated margarine   *5 ml/1 tsp vanilla essence*
15 ml/1 tbsp water   *50 g/2 oz raisins*
    1 egg, beaten

Heat the oven to 200°C/400°F/gas 6.
    Mix together the oats, flour and sugar. Melt the margarine with
the water, then add to the dry ingredients, mixing well. Press into
the base and sides of a 20 cm/8 inch flan tin. Bake for 20 minutes
until lightly browned.
    Beat together the cheese, sugar, vanilla, raisins and egg. Pour
into the flan case. Reduce the oven heat to 160°C/325°F/gas 3 and
bake the cheesecake for 20–25 minutes until just set. Leave to
cool, then remove from the tin.

Clootie dumpling

Serves 8
Per serving: 384 kcal, 1616 KJ, 8.5 g protein, 14.2 g fat,
59 g carbohydrate, 1.2 g soluble fibre, 2.6 g insoluble fibre

The original Scottish clootie dumpling was steamed in a cloth for
hours but it works very well baked and is quicker to cook too.

100 g/4 oz fine oatmeal
225 g/8 oz self-raising wholewheat
  flour
75 g/3 oz soft dark brown sugar
225 g/8 oz mixed dried fruit
10 ml/2 tsp ground cinnamon

10 ml/2 tsp ground ginger
100 g/4 oz vegetable suet
30 ml/2 tbsp clear honey
3 eggs, beaten
90 ml/6 tbsp milk

Heat the oven to 180°C/350°F/gas 4.
    Mix together the oatmeal, flour, sugar, fruit, spices and suet.
Make a well in the centre and add the honey, eggs and milk. Beat
well to mix thoroughly. Turn into a greased 1.5 litre/2½ pint
ovenproof dish and cover with foil. Place the dish in a roasting tin,
then add hot water to the tin to come halfway up the dish. Bake
the pudding for 1½ hours until firm to the touch. Serve warm
with custard.

Apple parkin pudding

Serves 6
Per serving: 583 kcal, 2448 KJ, 8.4 g protein, 27.2 g fat,
81.1 g carbohydrate, 2.2 g soluble fibre, 3.7 g insoluble fibre

175 g/6 oz polyunsaturated margarine
100 g/4 oz golden granulated sugar
75 g/3 oz golden syrup
50 g/2 oz black treacle
75 ml/3 fl oz milk
7.5 ml/1½ tsp bicarbonate of soda

175 g/6 oz wholewheat flour
175 g/6 oz rolled oats
10 ml/2 tsp ground ginger
450 g/1 lb cooking apples, peeled and
  thinly sliced

Heat the oven to 160°C/325°F/gas 3.
    Place the margarine, half the sugar, the syrup and treacle in a
large saucepan. Heat gently until the margarine has melted, then
remove from the heat and stir in the milk and bicarbonate of soda.
Add the flour, oats and ginger, stirring well.
    Arrange the apple slices in the base of a 1.8 litre/3 pint greased
ovenproof dish. Sprinkle with the remaining sugar and cover
evenly with the parkin mixture. Bake for 1–1¼ hours until firm to
the touch. Cool in the dish for 10 minutes, then turn out and
serve warm.

Mincemeat and apple tart

Serves 6
Per serving: 289 kcal, 1278 KJ, 3.1 g protein, 12.7 g fat,
47.1 g carbohydrate, 6.4 g soluble fibre, 6.2 g insoluble fibre

50 g/2 oz fine oatmeal
75 g/3 oz self-raising wholewheat
  flour
25 g/1 oz light muscovado sugar
75 g/3 oz polyunsaturated margarine

30 ml/2 tbsp water
2 medium cooking apples, peeled and
  finely chopped
225 g/8 oz mincemeat

Heat the oven to 190°C/375°F/gas 5.

Place the oatmeal, flour and sugar in a bowl. Add the margarine, in small pieces, and rub in with the fingertips until the mixture resembles breadcrumbs. Add the water and mix to a firm dough. Knead lightly on a floured surface then roll out and line a 23 cm/9 inch flan tin. Trim the edges of the pastry, reserving the trimmings.

Mix together the apples and mincemeat and spread over the pastry case. Roll out the pastry trimmings and cut into small rounds using a fluted cutter. Place over the filling. Bake for 35–40 minutes until the pastry is crisp and golden brown. Serve warm or cold.

Apple layer pudding

Serves 6   See photograph, page 92
Per serving: 289 kcal, 1231 KJ, 3.5 g protein, 12.8 g fat,
35.7 g carbohydrate, 1.7 g soluble fibre, 1.9 g insoluble fibre

75 g/3 oz butter or polyunsaturated
  margarine
175 g/6 oz rolled oats
75 g/3 oz demerara sugar
5 ml/1 tsp cinnamon

675 g/1½ lb cooking apples, peeled,
  cored and sliced
15 ml/1 tbsp lemon juice
60 ml/4 tbsp raspberry seedless jam
150 ml/¼ Greek yoghurt
25 g/1 oz grated chocolate

Melt the butter or margarine in a large pan, add the oats and fry, stirring for 5 minutes until lightly browned. Stir in 50 g/2 oz of the sugar and the cinnamon and leave to cool.

Cook the apples in a covered pan with the lemon juice and a little water until soft and pulpy. Beat until smooth, then stir in the remaining sugar.

Sprinkle one-third of the oats into a glass serving bowl. Spread over half the apple purée and half the jam. Sprinkle over half the remaining oats. Spread with the remaining apple and jam and finish with a layer of oats. Spread the yoghurt over the top and sprinkle with chocolate. Chill before serving.

Orange oat pudding

Serves 6
Per serving: 290 kcal, 1219 KJ, 5 g protein, 12.8 g fat,
41.4 g carbohydrate, 1.3 g soluble fibre, 1.6 g insoluble fibre

30 ml/2 tbsp golden syrup
2 oranges
75 g/3 oz medium oatmeal
75 g/3 oz self-raising wholewheat
 flour
2.5 ml/½ tsp baking powder

75 g/3 oz vegetable suet
50 g/2 oz soft brown sugar
75 g/3 oz raisins
1 egg, beaten
60 ml/4 tbsp milk

Heat the syrup in a small pan, then increase the heat and boil for 2 minutes until golden brown. Pour into a greased 900 ml/1½ pint pudding basin and swirl round quickly to coat the base and side.

Grate the rind from the oranges and reserve. Remove all the peel and white pith from the oranges. Cut the oranges into thin slices and press around the base and sides of the basin.

Place the oatmeal, flour, baking powder and suet in a bowl and mix well. Stir in the sugar and raisins. Make a well in the centre and add the egg and milk. Beat lightly to a soft consistency. Transfer the mixture carefully to the basin and smooth the top. Cover with double thickness, buttered greaseproof paper and tie down. Steam the pudding for 1½ hours, then remove and turn out. Serve immediately with thick natural yoghurt sweetened with a little honey.

Spiced oatmeal crumble

Serves 6
Per serving: 284 kcal, 1197 KJ, 4.1 g protein, 11.3 g fat,
44.4 g carbohydrate, 0.9 g soluble fibre, 1.7 g insoluble fibre

450–675 g/1–1½ lb fresh fruit such
 as rhubarb, apple, gooseberries,
 plums
50 g/2 oz soft light brown sugar
15 ml/1 tbsp lemon juice

Crumble:
100 g/4 oz wholewheat flour
50 g/2 oz medium oatmeal
10 ml/2 tsp mixed spice
75 g/3 oz butter or polyunsaturated
 margarine
50 g/2 oz soft light brown sugar

Heat the oven to 190°C/375°F/gas 5.

Prepare the fruit and place in a buttered 1.2 litre/2 pint oven-proof dish. Sprinkle over the sugar, lemon juice and 45–60 ml/3–4 tbsp water.

Place the flour, oatmeal and spice in a bowl. Add the margarine, in small pieces, and rub in with the fingertips until the mixture resembles fine breadcrumbs. Stir in the sugar. Sprinkle evenly over the fruit and bake for 30–35 minutes until the crumble is crispy and browned. Serve warm with ice cream or yoghurt.

Plum flapjack tart

Serves 6
Per serving: 180 kcal, 757 KJ, 2.6 g protein, 10.7 g fat,
19.7 g carbohydrate, 1.8 g soluble fibre, 1.3 g insoluble fibre

Pastry:
125 g/5 oz plain flour
25 g/1 oz medium oatmeal
5 ml/1 tsp ground cinnamon
75 g/3 oz polyunsaturated margarine
15–30 ml/1–2 tbsp cold water, to mix

Filling and topping:
450 g/1 lb plums, stoned and chopped
60 ml/4 tbsp golden syrup
40 g/1½ oz soft brown sugar
40 g/1½ oz polyunsaturated margarine
75 g/3 oz rolled oats

Heat the oven to 200°C/400°F/gas 6.

Mix the flour, oatmeal and cinnamon in a bowl. Add the margarine, in small pieces, and rub in with the fingertips until the mixture resembles fine breadcrumbs. Add 15–30 ml/1–2 tbsp cold water and mix to form a firm dough. Knead lightly, then roll out and line a 20 cm/8 inch pie plate. Pinch the edges with the fingers to decorate. Fill the pastry case with plums.

Heat together the syrup, sugar and margarine until the margarine has melted. Do not boil. Stir in the oats lightly, then spread the mixture over the plums. Bake for 35–40 minutes until the pastry and topping are golden brown. Serve warm.

Cream crowdie

Serves 4
Per serving: 336 kcal, 1395 KJ, 3.5 g protein, 27.1 g fat,
20.8 g carbohydrate, 0.5 g soluble fibre, 0.4 g insoluble fibre

This is a traditional recipe but it is high in fat and is best reserved for special occasions.

50 g/2 oz medium oatmeal
150 ml/¼ pint single cream
150 ml/¼ pint double cream
25 g/1 oz caster sugar

2.5 ml/½ tsp vanilla essence
225 g/8 oz fresh or frozen and thawed
   raspberries

Toast the oatmeal on a tray in the oven or under a moderate grill until lightly browned. Reserve a little for decoration.

Whip the creams together until thick. Fold in the sugar and vanilla essence, followed by the oatmeal and raspberries. Divide the mixture between four glasses and serve as soon as possible. Sprinkle a little reserved oatmeal over the top of each serving.

Citrus pear loaf (see page 108); Lunchbox squares (see page 109). OVERLEAF Oaty carrot cake (*above left*, see page 111); Fruit and nut crunchies (*below left*, see page 118); Oaty-topped scones (*centre and above right*, see page 117); Oatmeal soda bread (*right*, see page 116).

Raisin and almond flan

Serves 6
Per serving: 494 kcal, 2062 KJ, 7.3 g protein, 32.2 g fat,
46.6 g carbohydrate, 1.3 g soluble fibre, 2.8 g insoluble fibre

1 quantity High Fibre Pastry, see
  page 120
100 g/4 oz polyunsaturated margarine
100 g/4 oz soft light brown sugar

1 egg beaten
75 g/3 oz ground almonds
100 g/4 oz raisins
few drops almond essence

Heat the oven to 200°C/400°F/gas 6.
  Roll out the pastry and line a 20 cm/8 inch flan tin. Beat
together the fat and sugar until light and fluffy. Add the egg and
almonds, mixing well. Stir in the raisins and almond essence and
spread over the pastry case. Bake for 20 minutes, then reduce the
oven temperature to 180°C/350°F/gas 4 and bake for a further 20–
25 minutes until the filling is firm and golden brown.

Oaty strawberry shortcake

Serves 6
Per serving: 324 kcal, 1358 KJ, 11.9 g protein, 15.8 g fat,
35.7 g carbohydrate, 1.3 g soluble fibre, 1 g insoluble fibre

175 g/6 oz self-raising flour
50 g/2 oz medium oatmeal
2.5 ml/½ tsp ground cinnamon
50 g/2 oz polyunsaturated margarine
1 egg, beaten
45 ml/3 tbsp milk

175 g/6 oz unflavoured fromage
  blanc
15 ml/1 tbsp caster sugar
225 g/8 oz strawberries
10 ml/2 tsp icing sugar, to dust

Heat the oven to 200°C/400°F/gas 6.
  Mix the flour, oatmeal and cinnamon in a bowl. Add the
margarine in small pieces and rub in with the fingertips. Add the
egg and milk and mix quickly and lightly to a soft dough. Knead
the dough briefly, then shape into an 18 cm/7 inch round. Place
on a baking sheet and mark the top into six wedges. Bake for 20–
25 minutes, until well risen and golden brown. Cool on a wire
rack, then slice in half horizontally.
  Mix the fromage blanc and caster sugar. Reserve one whole
strawberry and slice the remainder. Arrange the sliced strawberries over the base of the shortcake and spread the fromage
blanc over the top.
  Break the top half of the shortcake into six wedges. Arrange
over the top of the filling, at an angle and slightly overlapping.
Place the reserved strawberry in the centre and dust with sifted
icing sugar.

Oaty strawberry shortcake (*above*); Oatmeal pancakes (*below*, see
page 106).

Oatmeal pancakes

Makes 8   See photograph, page 104
Per pancake: 91 kcal, 385 KJ, 3.4 g protein, 3.9 g fat,
11.3 g carbohydrate, 0.3 g soluble fibre, 0.3 g insoluble fibre

50 g/2 oz plain flour   *300 ml/½ pint semi-skimmed milk*
50 g/2 oz fine oatmeal   *15 ml/1 tbsp sunflower oil*
1 egg

Mix the flour and oatmeal in a bowl. Make a well in the centre and
drop in the egg. Gradually beat in half the milk until the mixture is
smooth. Stir in the remaining milk. Brush a 20 cm/8 inch frying
pan with a little oil and heat until hot, then reduce heat. Pour in a
little batter, swirling the pan to cover it thinly. When the pancake
is lightly browned on the underside, turn it with a palette knife
and cook on the other side. Keep warm while cooking the rest of
the pancakes. Wrap around any savoury or fruit filling, or serve
with lemon juice and a little honey.

Apple and raisin crumble squares

Makes 15
Per square: 174 kcal, 733 KJ, 2.6 g protein, 6.2 g fat,
28.7 g carbohydrate, 0.8 g soluble fibre, 1.4 g insoluble fibre

450 g/1 lb cooking apples, peeled,   Crumble:
  quartered and cored   *175 g/6 oz wholewheat flour*
100 g/4 oz raisins   *100 g/4 oz medium oatmeal*
5 ml/1 tsp finely grated orange rind   *100 g/4 oz polyunsaturated margarine*
45 ml/3 tbsp orange juice   *75 g/3 oz soft light brown sugar*
45 ml/3 tbsp water
50 g/2 oz soft light brown sugar

Heat the oven to 190°C/375°F/gas 5.
    Slice the apples then place in a pan with the raisins, orange rind
and juice and water. Simmer, uncovered, for about 10 minutes
until pulpy. Remove from the heat and stir in the sugar. Cool.
    Place the flour and oatmeal in a bowl. Add the margarine, cut
into small pieces and rub in with the fingertips until the mixture
resembles breadcrumbs. Stir in the sugar. Sprinkle half the mixture over the base of a greased 28 cm × 18 cm/11 × 7 inch shallow
tin. Press down lightly. Spread the apple mixture evenly over the
top. Cover with the remaining crumble mixture and press down
lightly. Bake for 35 minutes until lightly browned. Leave to cool
in the tin, then cut into three down length and five across. Serve
warm or cold.

Apple oat pudding

Serves 6
Per serving: 478 kcal, 2011 KJ, 6.8 g protein, 19.8 fat,
72.6 g carbohydrate, 1.8 g soluble fibre, 1.3 g insoluble fibre

450 g/1 lb cooking apples, peeled,
* cored and thinly sliced*
15 ml/1 tbsp lemon juice
175 g/6 oz soft brown sugar
125 g/5 oz self-raising wholewheat
* flour*

175 g/6 oz rolled oats
10 ml/2 tsp ground cinnamon
125 g/5 oz butter or polyunsaturated
* margarine, melted*

Heat the oven to 180°C/350°F/gas 4.

Place the apples in a bowl with the lemon juice and 50 g/2 oz of
the sugar and turn gently until the apple slices are evenly coated
with the sugar.

Place the remaining sugar in a bowl with the flour, oats and
cinnamon. Mix well. Pour in the melted butter or margarine and
mix thoroughly. Sprinkle half this mixture evenly over the base of
a greased 20 cm/8 inch loose-based cake tin. Press down lightly
with the back of a spoon. Arrange the apple slices over the top and
pour any juices over them. Sprinkle the remaining oat mixture
over the apples and press down lightly. Bake for 35–40 minutes
until the top of the pudding is golden brown. Carefully remove
from the tin and serve warm or cold.

Rhubarb and ginger crumble

Serves 4
Per serving: 326 kcal, 1371 KJ, 4.5 g protein, 14.5 g fat,
47.3 g carbohydrate, 1.7 g soluble fibre, 2 g insoluble fibre

450 g/1 lb rhubarb, chopped
50 g/2 oz soft brown sugar
25 g/1 oz preserved stem ginger,
* chopped*
60 ml/4 tbsp orange juice

100 g/4 oz rolled oats
50 g/2 oz demerara sugar
50 g/2 oz polyunsaturated margarine
25 g/1 oz chopped hazelnuts

Heat the oven to 190°C/375°F/gas 5.

Mix the rhubarb, soft brown sugar, ginger and orange juice.
Place in a 1.2 litre/2 pint ovenproof dish.

Mix the oats and sugar. Add the margarine in small pieces and
rub in with the fingertips. Stir in the nuts. Sprinkle the crumble
over the fruit and bake for 35–45 minutes, until the topping is
browned and the rhubarb is tender.

CAKES
AND BAKING

Citrus pear loaf

Makes 12 slices   See photograph, page 101
Per serving: 159 kcal, 669 KJ, 4.4 g protein, 6.5 g fat,
22.3 g carbohydrate, 1.9 g soluble fibre, 2.8 g insoluble fibre

5 ml/1 tsp allspice
175 g/6 oz self-raising wholewheat
  flour
50 g/2 oz rolled oats
5 ml/1 tsp baking powder
75 g/3 oz polyunsaturated margarine

50 g/2 oz soft dark brown sugar
175 g/6 oz dried pears, chopped
1 orange, about 100 g/4 oz
1 egg, beaten
300 ml/½ pint natural low-fat
  yoghurt

Heat the oven to 160°C/325°F/gas 3.

Mix the allspice, flour, oats and baking powder in a bowl. Add the margarine, in small pieces, and rub in until the mixture resembles fine breadcrumbs. Stir in the sugar and pears. Finely grate the rind from the orange and stir in. Remove all the remaining rind and white pith from the orange. Cut the orange into thin slices and reserve.

Add the egg and yoghurt to the dry mixture and mix to form a soft mixture. Turn into a greased and base-lined 900 g/2 lb loaf tin and smooth the top. Arrange the orange slices overlapping along the top. Bake for 1 hour until firm to the touch. Cool in the tin for 10 minutes, then turn out and cool on a wire rack. Serve thinly sliced.

Fruit tea brack

Makes 12 slices
Per slice: 189 kcal, 802 KJ, 4.6 g protein, 2.3 g fat,
39.9 g carbohydrate, 0.9 g soluble fibre, 1.8 g insoluble fibre

275 g/10 mixed dried fruit
75 g/3 oz soft brown sugar
grated rind ½ lemon
350 ml/12 fl oz hot tea
225 g/8 oz self-raising wholewheat flour

100 g/4 oz medium oatmeal
10 ml/2 tsp mixed spice
5 ml/1 tsp baking powder
1 egg, beaten
25 g/1 oz chopped nuts, for topping

Heat the oven to 190°C/375°F/gas 5.

Place the fruit, sugar, lemon rind and tea in a bowl, and mix well. Leave to soak overnight or for at least 4 hours. Stir in the flour, oatmeal, spice, baking powder and egg and mix well. Turn the mixture into a greased and base-lined 900 g/2 lb loaf tin and smooth the top. Sprinkle the nuts over the top. Bake for 45–50 minutes until well risen and firm to the touch. Turn out and cool on a wire rack. Serve thinly sliced.

Lunchbox squares

Makes 12   See photograph, page 101
Per square: 212 kcal, 885 KJ, 3.3 g protein, 12.3 g fat,
23.3 g carbohydrate, 0.6 soluble fibre, 1 g insoluble fibre

100 g/4 oz polyunsaturated margarine
100 g/4 oz soft light brown sugar
1 egg, beaten
5 ml/1 tsp vanilla essence
75 g/3 oz rolled oats

75 g/3 oz wholewheat flour
100 g/4 oz stoned dates, chopped
100 g/4 oz walnuts, chopped
45 ml/3 tbsp milk

Heat the oven to 180°C/350°F/gas 4.

Beat together the margarine, sugar, egg and vanilla, for about 3 minutes. Stir in the oats and flour. Lightly mix in the dates, walnuts and milk. Transfer to a greased 18 cm/7 inch square tin. Bake for 25–30 minutes, until lightly browned and firm to the touch. Cool in the tin for 10 minutes, then cut into three one way and four the other. Remove from the tin and cool on a wire rack.

Almond oat squares

Makes 9
Per square: 233 kcal, 970 KJ, 3.4 g protein, 15.9 g fat,
20.2 g carbohydrate, 0.9 g soluble fibre, 0.9 insoluble fibre

125 g/4 oz polyunsaturated margarine   *50 g/2 oz ground almonds*
175 g/6 oz jumbo oats   *few drops almond essence*
50 g/2 oz soft brown sugar   *2.5 ml/½ tsp grated orange rind*

Heat the oven to 180°C/350°F/gas 4.

Melt the margarine in a saucepan. Remove from heat and stir in all the remaining ingredients, mixing thoroughly. Turn into a greased 18 cm/7 inch square tin and smooth the top with the back of a spoon. Bake for 30 minutes until the top is crisp and golden. Cool in the tin for 5 minutes, then cut into three each way to make nine squares.

Nutty oat biscuits

Makes 20
Per biscuit: 109 kcal, 456 KJ, 1.5 g protein, 6.6 g fat,
11.7 g carbohydrate, 0.3 g soluble fibre, 0.6 g insoluble fibre

75 g/3 oz wholewheat flour   *5 ml/1 tsp bicarbonate of soda*
100 g/4 oz soft light brown sugar   *30 ml/2 tbsp honey*
25 g/1 oz desiccated coconut   *100 g/4 oz polyunsaturated margarine*
75 g/3 oz rolled oats   *halved almonds or walnuts*
25 g/1 oz chopped nuts

Heat the oven to 180°C/350°F/gas 4.

Mix together the flour, sugar, coconut, oats, nuts and bicarbonate of soda in a mixing bowl.

Heat together the honey and margarine in a small pan until melted. Add to the dry ingredients and mix well. Shape into balls about 2.5 cm/1 inch across and place a little apart on greased baking sheets. Press half a nut into each. Bake for 12–15 minutes until golden brown. Cool for a couple of minutes, then remove from the baking sheets and cool on a wire rack. Store in a tin.

Digestive biscuits

Makes 30
Per biscuit: 81 kcal, 340 KJ, 1.4 g protein, 4.6 g fat,
9 g carbohydrate, 0.3 g soluble fibre, 0.4 g insoluble fibre

100 g/4 oz plain flour
100 g/4 oz wholewheat flour
100 g/4 oz fine oatmeal

150 g/5 oz polyunsaturated margarine
50 g/2 oz soft light brown sugar
1 egg, beaten

Heat the oven to 180°C/350°F/gas 4.

Mix the flours and oatmeal in a bowl. Add the margarine in small pieces and rub in with the fingertips until the mixture resembles breadcrumbs.

Mix in the sugar, then add the egg and 45–60 ml/3–4 tbsp cold water and mix to form a firm dough.

Knead the dough lightly, then roll out thinly on a lightly floured surface. Cut into rounds with an 8 cm/3 inch cutter and transfer to greased baking sheets. Prick the biscuits all over and bake for 25 minutes, until lightly browned. Cool on a wire rack.

Oaty carrot cake

Makes 12 slices   See photograph, page 102
Per slice: 355 kcal, 1487 KJ, 7.1 g protein, 22.6 g fat,
32.6 g carbohydrate, 0.7 g soluble fibre, 1.2 g insoluble fibre

175 g/6 oz soft brown sugar
175 ml/6 fl oz sunflower oil
3 eggs, beaten
225 g/8 oz carrots, grated
100 g/4 oz raisins
50 g/2 oz hazelnuts
100 g/4 oz self-raising wholewheat
  flour
50 g/2 oz rolled oats

5 ml/1 tsp bicarbonate of soda
5 ml/1 tsp cinnamon
2.5 ml/½ tsp nutmeg

Frosting:
225 g/8 oz curd cheese
10 ml/2 tsp lemon juice
25 g/1 oz icing sugar, sifted

Heat the oven to 180°C/350°F/gas 4.

Place the sugar, oil and eggs in a bowl and mix together lightly. Stir in the carrots, raisins and hazelnuts. Mix together the flour, oats, bicarbonate of soda and spices. Add to the bowl, mixing lightly until evenly blended. Turn into a greased and base-lined 20 cm/8 inch square tin. Bake for 35–40 minutes until firm to the touch. Turn out and cool on a wire rack.

Beat together the frosting ingredients and spread over the top of the cake. Serve cut into squares.

Chocolate flapjack

Makes 15 pieces
Per piece: 161 kcal, 675 KJ, 2.1 g protein, 7.7 g fat,
22.3 g carbohydrate, 0.5 g soluble fibre, 0.4 g insoluble fibre

125 g/4 oz polyunsaturated margarine   *75 g/3 oz soft brown sugar*
50 g/2 oz plain chocolate, broken up   *225 g/8 oz rolled oats*
75 g/3 oz golden syrup

Heat the oven to 180°C/350°F/gas 4.

Place the margarine, chocolate, syrup and sugar in a saucepan. Heat gently, stirring, until the margarine and chocolate have melted and the mixture is smooth. Remove from the heat and stir in the oats until they are thoroughly coated.

Press the mixture into a greased 18 × 28 cm/7 × 11 inch shallow oblong tin and smooth the top. Bake for 20 minutes until the top is slightly crispy. Cool in the tin for 5 minutes, then cut into three down length and five across to make fifteen pieces. Cool on a wire rack.

Applesauce oat cake

Makes 8 slices
Per slice: 353 kcal, 1483 KJ, 5.5 g protein, 17.7 g fat,
45.7 g carbohydrate, 1 g soluble fibre, 2.1 g insoluble fibre

150 g/5 oz self-raising wholewheat   *225 g/8 oz apple purée*
   flour   *75 g/3 oz stoned dates, chopped*
75 g/3 oz rolled oats   *2 eggs, beaten*
5 ml/1 tsp baking powder   *15 ml/1 tbsp demerara sugar, to*
5 ml/1 tsp ground ginger   *sprinkle*
150 g/5 oz polyunsaturated margarine   *15 ml/1 tbsp rolled oats, to sprinkle*
100 g/4 oz soft light brown sugar

Heat the oven to 190°C/375°F/gas 5.

Mix the flour, oats, baking powder and ginger in a bowl. Add the margarine, in small pieces, and rub in with the fingertips until thoroughly incorporated. Stir in the sugar, apple purée, dates and eggs. Stir together until well mixed.

Turn the mixture into a greased and lined 18 cm/7 inch round cake tin and smooth the top. Sprinkle with the demerara sugar and oats. Bake for 1–1¼ hours until firm to the touch. Cool in the tin for 10 minutes, then turn out and cool on a wire rack.

Highland broonie loaf

Makes 10 slices
Per slice: 239 kcal, 1009 KJ, 5.4 g protein, 8.8 g fat,
36.8 g carbohydrate, 1 g soluble fibre, 1.7 g insoluble fibre

175 g/6 oz wholewheat flour
10 ml/2 tsp ground ginger
5 ml/1 tsp baking powder
175 g/6 oz medium oatmeal
75 g/3 oz polyunsaturated margarine

100 g/4 oz soft dark brown sugar
30 ml/2 tbsp black treacle
250–300 ml/8–10 fl oz buttermilk
1 egg, beaten

Heat the oven to 180°C/350°F/gas 4.

Mix the flour, ginger, baking powder and oatmeal in a bowl. Add the margarine, in small pieces, and rub in with the fingertips until the mixture resembles fine breadcrumbs. Stir in the sugar.

Warm the treacle a little, then stir in half the buttermilk and the egg. Stir this into the dry ingredients, adding more buttermilk until a soft dropping batter is formed. Pour the mixture into a greased and base-lined 900 g/2 lb loaf tin and bake for 1–1¼ hours until well risen and firm to the touch. Cool in the tin for 10 minutes, then turn out and cool on a wire rack. Serve sliced and buttered if you like.

Apple oat slices

Makes 15 pieces
Per slice: 133 kcal, 560 KJ, 1.8 g protein, 6.6 g fat,
17.9 g carbohydrate, 0.6 g soluble fibre, 0.9 g insoluble fibre

100 g/4 oz self-raising wholewheat flour
75 g/3 oz rolled oats
100 g/4 oz polyunsaturated margarine
25 g/1 oz soft brown sugar

450 g/1 lb cooking apples, peeled, cored and thinly sliced
75 g/3 oz raisins
25 g/1 oz hazelnuts
25 g/1 oz demerara sugar
5 ml/1 tsp cinnamon

Heat the oven to 190°C/375°F/gas 5.

Mix the flour and oats together in a bowl. Add the margarine, in small pieces, and rub in with the fingertips. Stir in the sugar and draw the mixture together until it forms a dough. Add a little water if necessary. Press the mixture into a greased 33 cm×22 cm/ 13 × 9 inch shallow tin.

Arrange apple slices over the dough and sprinkle with raisins, nuts, sugar and cinnamon. Bake for 35–40 minutes until the apples are tender. Cool slightly before cutting into wedges. Serve warm or cold.

Sesame oat bars

Makes 18
Per serving: 113 kcal, 474 KJ, 1.8 g protein, 7.6 g fat,
10.2 g carbohydrate, 0.4 g soluble fibre, 0.4 g insoluble fibre

45 ml/3 tbsp clear honey   *50 g/2 oz chopped nuts*
100 g/4 oz polyunsaturated margarine *125 g/5 oz coarse oatmeal*
50 g/2 oz soft light brown sugar *50 g/2 oz sesame seeds*

Heat the oven to 180°C/350°F/gas 4.
 Place the honey, margarine and sugar in a saucepan. Heat gently until the margarine has melted. Stir in the nuts, oatmeal and sesame seeds and mix well. Press into a greased 28 cm × 18 cm/11 × 7 inch shallow tin. Bake for 20 minutes until lightly browned. Cool in the tin for a few minutes, then cut into three down length and six across to make bars.

Oaten plait

Makes 10 slices
Per slice: 158 kcal, 671 KJ, 5.5 g protein, 2.5 g fat,
30.1 g carbohydrate, 1 g soluble fibre, 1.5 g insoluble fibre

5 ml/1 tsp sugar   *325 g/12 oz 85% brown flour*
10 ml/2 tsp dried yeast *100 g/4 oz rolled oats*
300 ml/½ pint warm water *10 ml/2 tsp sunflower oil*
5 ml/1 tsp salt   *oats, to sprinkle*

Sprinkle the sugar and yeast into the warm water and leave for 10 minutes, until frothy.
 Place all the remaining ingredients in a large bowl. Make a well in the centre and pour in the yeast liquid. Mix well to form a soft dough. Knead well on a lightly floured surface for 5 minutes until the dough is no longer sticky. Divide into three equal pieces and pinch the strands together at one end. Plait loosely and pinch the ends together. Place on a greased baking sheet, brush with water and sprinkle with oats. Cover with oiled polythene and leave to rise for 40–50 minutes until the dough is well risen and springs back when pressed.
 Heat the oven to 220°C/425°F/gas 7 and bake for 30–35 minutes until well browned and the loaf sounds hollow when tapped on the base. Cool on a wire rack.

American oat cookies

Makes 16 large cookies
Per cookie: 222 kcal, 931 KJ, 3 g protein, 10.5 g fat,
30.5 g carbohydrate, 0.7 g soluble fibre, 0.9 g insoluble fibre

175 g/6 oz polyunsaturated margarine
225 g/8 oz soft brown sugar
1 egg, beaten
15 ml/1 tbsp water
5 ml/1 tsp vanilla essence
30 ml/2 tbsp golden syrup
100 g/4 oz wholewheat flour
5 ml/1 tsp cinnamon
2.5 ml/½ tsp bicarbonate of soda
225 g/8 oz rolled oats

Heat the oven to 180°C/350°F/gas 4.

Beat together the margarine and sugar until light and fluffy, about 10 minutes. Beat in the egg, water, vanilla and syrup. Sift the flour, cinnamon and bicarbonate of soda into the bowl. Lightly mix in using a metal spoon, then add the oats, mixing until they are evenly blended in.

Place tablespoonfuls of mixture, well apart, on greased baking sheets. Bake for 12–15 minutes until lightly browned. Cool on a wire rack. The biscuits will be chewy in the centre.

Honey oat squares

Makes 9
Per square: 198 kcal, 828 KJ, 2.4 g protein, 10.8 g fat,
24.2 g carbohydrate, 0.6 g soluble fibre, 0.5 g insoluble fibre

75 g/3 oz polyunsaturated margarine
60 ml/4 tbsp clear honey
75 g/3 oz soft brown sugar
125 g/5 oz rolled oats
50 g/2 oz chopped walnuts

Heat the oven to 180°C/350°F/gas 4.

Place the margarine and honey in a medium-size saucepan and heat until the margarine has melted. Remove from heat and stir in the sugar and oats. Mix well. Spread evenly over a greased 18 cm/7 inch square tin. Sprinkle with the walnuts and press down lightly. Bake for 25–30 minutes until golden brown. Cool in the tin for 10 minutes, then cut into nine squares. Cool completely in the tin.

Oatmeal soda bread

Makes 1 large or 2 small loaves   See photograph, page 103
Per small loaf: 1213 kcal, 5155 KJ, 45.2 g protein, 15.9 g fat,
237.2 g carbohydrate, 8.8 g soluble fibre, 14.3 g insoluble fibre

500 g/1 lb 2 oz 85% brown flour   *5 ml/1 tsp salt*
175 g/6 oz fine oatmeal   *600 ml/1 pint buttermilk*
5 ml/1 tsp bicarbonate of soda   *oatmeal, to sprinkle*

Heat the oven to 200°C/400°F/gas 6.
   Mix the flour and oatmeal in a large bowl. Add the bicarbonate
of soda, breaking up any lumps with the fingers. Mix it into the
flour thoroughly with the hands. Stir in the salt.
   Add the buttermilk, all at once, and mix lightly and quickly to
form a soft dough. Knead very briefly, then shape into one large
round or two smaller ones. Place on a baking sheet dusted with
flour. Sprinkle the top with oatmeal and bake for 30–35 minutes
until the bread is well browned and sounds hollow when tapped on
the base. Cool on a wire rack.

Quick buttermilk bread

Makes 2 small loaves, 8 wedges per loaf
Per wedge: 149 kcal, 635 KJ, 5.3 g protein, 1.5 g fat,
30.4 g carbohydrate, 1 g soluble fibre, 2 g insoluble fibre

350 g/12 oz wholewheat flour   *5 ml/1 tsp salt*
225 g/8 oz plain flour   *600 ml/1 pint buttermilk*
100 g/4 oz rolled oats   *oats, to sprinkle*
5 ml/1 tsp bicarbonate of soda

Heat the oven to 200°C/400°F/gas 6.
   Mix the flours and oats in a mixing bowl. Add the bicarbonate of
soda and salt, rubbing them through your fingers to break up any
lumps. Mix well.
   Add the buttermilk, all at once, and mix quickly to form a soft
dough. Add a little milk if the dough seems dry. Knead the dough
very briefly, then divide in half and shape each piece into a round.
Place the rounds on a floured baking sheet and cut a deep cross in
the top of each one. Sprinkle with oats and bake for 30 minutes
until they are browned and sound hollow when tapped on the
base. Cool on a wire rack.

Oatmeal scones

Makes 8
Per scone: 172 kcal, 725 KJ, 4.2 g protein, 6.8 g fat,
25.1 g carbohydrate, 0.6 soluble fibre, 1.5 g insoluble fibre

*150 g/5 oz self-raising wholewheat
    flour
75 g/3 oz fine oatmeal
10 ml/2 tsp baking powder*

*50 g/2 oz polyunsaturated margarine
40 g/1½ oz soft brown sugar
120 ml/8 tbsp milk*

Heat the oven to 220°C/425°F/gas 7.
    Mix together the flour, oatmeal and baking powder in a bowl.
Add the margarine, cut into small pieces, and rub in with the
fingertips until the mixture resembles fine breadcrumbs. Stir in
the sugar.
    Add the milk, all at once, and mix quickly and lightly to form a
soft dough. Knead briefly on a lightly floured surface then roll or
press out to a 20 cm/8 inch round. Cut across into eight wedges.
Place the wedges on a baking sheet, a little apart, and bake for 12–
15 minutes until well risen and browned. Cool on a wire rack.

Variations For Cheese Scones omit the sugar. Add 115 g/4 oz
finely grated Cheddar and 5 ml/1 tsp dry mustard to the rubbed-in
mixture. For Fruit Scones add 50 g/2 oz dried fruit to the rubbed-
in mixture.

Oaty-topped scones

Makes 10   See photograph, page 102
Per scone: 197 kcal, 831 KJ, 4.4 g protein, 6.9 g fat,
31.2 g carbohydrate, 0.6 g soluble fibre, 1.7 g insoluble fibre

*225 g/8 oz self-raising wholewheat
    flour
50 g/2 oz polyunsaturated margarine
50 g/2 oz rolled oats
75 g/3 oz soft light brown sugar
150 ml/¼ pint milk*

Topping:
*30 ml/2 tbsp golden syrup
15 g/½ oz polyunsaturated margarine
25 g/1 oz rolled oats*

Heat the oven to 220°C/425°F/gas 7.
    Place the flour in a large bowl. Add the margarine, in small
pieces, and rub in until the mixture resembles breadcrumbs. Stir
in the oats and sugar. Add the milk and mix to form a soft dough.
Knead lightly and then roll out to a thickness of 2.5 cm/1 inch.
Dip cutter into flour before cutting dough into 10 rounds. Place
on a greased baking sheet.
    For the topping, gently heat the syrup and margarine in a small
pan. Remove from heat and stir in the oats. Spoon a teaspoonful
of the mixture on top of each scone. Bake for 12–15 minutes, until
the scones are well risen and golden brown.

Fruit and nut crunchies

Makes 20   See photograph, page 102
Per biscuit: 87 kcal, 367 KJ, 2.4 g protein, 4.5 g fat,
10.8 g carbohydrate, 0.4 g soluble fibre, 0.7 g insoluble fibre

1 egg   *50 g/2 oz dried figs*
100 g/4 oz soft dark brown sugar   *50 g/2 oz chopped nuts*
50 g/2 oz desiccated coconut   *50 g/2 oz sunflower seeds*
50 g/2 oz rolled oats   *5 ml/1 tsp ground cinnamon*
50 g/2 oz seedless raisins   *5 ml/1 tsp sunflower oil*

Heat the oven to 180°C/350°F/gas 4.
  Beat the egg and sugar together well. Add the remaining
ingredients and mix thoroughly. Place teaspoonfuls of the mixture, a little apart, on a greased baking sheet. Bake in the centre of
the oven for 15 minutes, until lightly browned and crispy at the
edges. Cool for 2 minutes on the baking sheet, then remove and
cool on a wire rack.

Fibre-rich shortbread

Makes 8 wedges
Per wedge: 262 kcal, 1089 KJ, 2.9 g protein, 18.8 g fat,
21.6 g carbohydrate, 1 g soluble fibre, 1.4 g insoluble fibre

175 g/6 oz butter or polyunsaturated   *100 g/4 oz plain wholewheat flour*
  margarine   *75 g/3 oz oat bran and oat germ*
50 g/2 oz soft brown sugar

Heat the oven to 160°C/325°F/gas 3.
  Cream the fat and sugar until light and fluffy, then add the flour
and oat bran and oat germ and mix until the dough clings
together. Knead lightly on a floured surface. Roll out and press
into a 20 cm/8 inch sandwich tin. Prick the shortbread all over
with a fork and bake for 30–40 minutes or until just lightly
browned. Mark the shortbread into eight wedges while still
warm.

Mincemeat flapjack

Makes 9 pieces
Per piece: 149 kcal, 632 KJ, 2.1 g protein, 8.4 g fat,
17.8 g carbohydrate, 0.7 g soluble fibre, 0.6 g insoluble fibre

75 g/3 oz polyunsaturated margarine   *45 ml/3 tbsp mincemeat*
30 ml/2 tbsp clear honey   *175 g/6 oz rolled oats*

Heat the oven to 160°C/325°F/gas 3.
    Place the margarine, honey and mincemeat in a saucepan. Heat
gently until the margarine has melted. Add the oats and stir well.
Press the mixture into a greased 18 cm/7 inch square shallow tin
and smooth the top with the back of a spoon. Bake for 25 minutes
until golden brown. Mark into three each way. Leave in the tin
until cool, then cut along marked lines.

Molasses oat bread

Makes 1 loaf, 10 slices
Per slice: 151 kcal, 641 KJ, 3.8 g protein, 2.7 g fat,
29.8 g carbohydrate, 0.9 g soluble fibre, 1.8 g insoluble fibre

15 g/½ oz dried yeast   *5 ml/1 tsp salt*
15 ml/1 tbsp soft brown sugar   *15 ml/1 tbsp sunflower oil*
175 ml/6 fl oz hand-hot water   *45 ml/3 tbsp molasses*
175 g/6 oz wholewheat flour   *100 g/4 oz stoned dates, chopped*
100 g/4 oz medium oatmeal

Sprinkle the yeast and sugar over the water and leave for 10
minutes, until frothy.
    Mix the flour, oatmeal and salt in a bowl. Add the oil and yeast
liquid and mix to a soft dough. Knead on a lightly floured surface
for about 10 minutes, until smooth and pliable. Cover and leave to
rise for about 1 hour. Knead again, gradually working in the
molasses and dates. Transfer to a greased 18 cm/7 inch cake tin,
cover and leave to rise for 1½ hours, until well risen.
    Heat the oven to 200°C/400°F/gas 6. Bake the bread for 30–35
minutes, until it sounds hollow when tapped on the base. Cool on
a wire rack.

High fibre pastry

Per quantity: 1097 kcal, 4851 KJ, 23.2 g protein, 66.8 g fat, 107.2 g carbohydrate, 5.7 g soluble fibre, 10.9 g insoluble fibre

*100 g/4 oz self-raising wholewheat
  flour*

*50 g/2 oz oat bran and oat germ
75 g/3 oz polyunsaturated margarine*

Mix together the flour and oat bran and oat germ in a mixing bowl. Add the margarine, in small pieces. Rub in with the fingertips until the mixture resembles fine breadcrumbs. Add 15–30 ml/ 1–2 tbsp cold water and mix to a firm dough. Turn out on to a lightly floured surface and knead lightly. Wrap in cling film and chill for 10 minutes before using.

ACKNOWLEDGMENTS

I would like to thank my family and friends for being such enthusiastic tasters of the recipes in this book. Their comments and criticisms were invaluable and greatly appreciated.

I am particularly grateful, as always, to Bob Mallon for all his encouragement. Thanks are also due to Jackie Eves, who typed all the recipes.

MC

I wish to thank Dr John Bond for his support and encouragement during the writing of the Introduction to this book and Margo Fletcher for typing the manuscript.

SB

The authors and publishers are grateful to Dr Hans Englyst of the Medical Research Council, Dunn Clinical Nutrition Centre, Cambridge, for supplying his figures for use in the soluble and insoluble dietary fibre analysis. The source for all the other nutritional analyses is McCance and Widdowson's *The Composition of Foods* (A.A. Paul and D.A.T. Southgate, HMSO).

Thanks are also due to Charlie Stebbings, who took the photographs, assisted by Mike Furze; Mary Cadogan and Clare Gordon-Smith for food preparation; Totty Whately for styling; and Morning Foods Ltd for supplying oat samples and sources of the black and white illustrations.

INDEX

Page numbers in *italic* refer to the illustrations